A Different Kind of Life

Christine Holmes

ISBN: 9798591460051

PublishNation
www.publishnation.co.uk

Introduction

This book is about those times in my life when I had to learn to depend on God. The times when loss and being broken was too much for me to carry. Times when my choices took me down paths that led to pain until truth began to dawn and the light of God offered a new beginning.

I grew up having a plan for my life and I had no reason to believe that it wouldn't happen the way I wanted it to. However, the reality of life is that plans have a habit of falling down when I least expect it. I'm left feeling puzzled as to why things happened the way they did. Life is such a learning curve and I've spent so much time feeling frustrated as I've struggled over situations in my life.

Facing loss can be devastating but leaning on God and learning to depend on him to get me through it became a lifeline. There was always something that I learnt that brought me closer to Jesus Christ. Life is what it is, there will always be good times and bad times but for the child of God every situation becomes something much deeper in relationship with him. He became my rock, my safe place and here he taught me to listen to his voice. That still small voice that speaks to the heart, reassuring me that I was never alone and never would be.

As a child I had all sorts of dreams for my life. None of my dreams came about the way I thought they would. Some never happened at all and some came with pain that I hadn't anticipated. Few came with happiness beyond anything I'd imagined. The twists and turns of life brought tears, laughter and often, lots of questions. So often I was the child who kept asking God, 'Why?'

Some people would tell me that I should never question God and just accept that he knew best, but I had a problem with that. I am curious, inquisitive and in everyday terms, plain nosey. Faced with a situation in life, I would be quiet and ponder it and then I'd pray in my safe place with God and usually begin with, 'I need to talk to you, we need to have a chat.' I wonder how other people speak to God. He knows me better than I know myself and before I even speak or do my usual walking up and down the floor in frustration, he is waiting for me to talk. I have been blessed with a sense of humour that only God can understand! I think he knew I would need it in life and at times when I laugh, I know he laughs with me. The beauty of a relationship with God is finding my real identity. He created me and in him I find the true meaning of life. I know who I belong to and that revelation brings a sense of belonging that is more valuable than any pearl of great value. However, my life hasn't always been like this. I had to go down a lot of dead-end paths, stumble in the dark, search for meaning in all the wrong places until finally I connected with God and light broke through. I often wonder, why on earth did it take me so long? But I got there, and it has been worth it.

As a child the story of Cinderella was my favourite. This poor girl who just wanted to be loved and accepted but was treated so badly by her step-sisters. Cinderella still held onto her dream for a better life and when the opportunity came for her to go to the ball, for one night she would feel like a princess. For one night her life would be different. For a few hours she would experience happiness and feel beautiful. And she did. When it ended, she knew she would always remember the joy of that one night.

But it wouldn't be for just one night because the prince came after her and her whole life changed when they fell in love and got married and lived happily ever after.

Now I know this is a fairy story, a beautiful one, but a story just the same. Yet as a child, I thought how amazing it would be to fall in love with a wonderful person and live happily ever after. To know a prince who would love me and protect me and guide me through life, drawing me to him for a relationship that would bring me joy and peace. Is there ever such a relationship as this? Hold that thought!

Real life is nothing like the fairy stories and it's not supposed to be. I think the clue is in the word, real! One day I questioned God about the way my life had turned out. In a moment of time I had glimpses of the past, good times and bad times and awful painful times and I was puzzled. In the stillness he told me that I'd had a different kind of life. I sighed; he was right about that. I replied that a different kind of life would be a good title for a book and suddenly I knew what I had to do. This book is about my different kind of life and how despite my choices I experienced a major comeback to God, and I have found peace in my soul. Each day his grace covers me. He taught me about having a relationship with him, and not religion.

I don't need to feel like I'm carrying the weight of the world on my shoulders because that is not what Jesus has for me. He invites me to come to him.

Matthew 11:28-30

Then Jesus said, 'Come to me, all of you who are weary and carry heavy burdens, and I will give you rest. Take my yoke upon you. Let me teach you, because I am humble and gentle at heart and you will find rest for your souls. For my yoke is easy to bear and the burden I give you is light.'

When circumstances close in on me and I've hit a wall, I know that the way forward is to be still in the Lord's presence and do exactly what he says, simply come to him. Jesus already knows everything about me, what troubles me and causes anxiety.

He knows the best way forward and he wants to teach me his way of doing things. My plans haven't always been his plans! Yet, his patience and love gently draws me back to where I should be.

My identity is in him, it's not in any other kind of relationship, or a career or a church. Most of all he is the Prince of Peace, but it would take years of life experience until I experienced that peace. Identity, the core of who I am is in Jesus Christ. I love my life because I am up close and personal in my relationship with Jesus. He cares about every detail of my life and I talk to him about everything that concerns me. Most of all a loving relationship with Jesus Christ is the rock-solid foundation on which my life is built. For me, there is no other way to live because it's the best. I am loved, secure and blessed and really, what more could a woman want?

Acts 17:28 N.L.T.

For in Him we live and move and exist. As some of your own poets have said, 'We are his offspring.'

Chapter 1

I was about four years old when I became aware of the world around me and my memory is noticeably clear about my surroundings. My family lived in a bungalow off the Shore Road in Belfast. I was told we moved there when I was a baby and at that time, I didn't have a cot, I had the bottom drawer of the chest of drawers in my parent's bedroom. We were like any other working-class family who managed as best they could with what they had.

In 1958 we moved from the Shore Road to a brand new three bedroomed house in Springfield Parade, off the Springfield Road. The houses were owned by the Belfast Corporation and there were quite a few new houses built although the area was still like a building site and the gardens non-existent. I was four years old and I remember the day we moved; the big furniture removal van had all our stuff packed onto it. I got to sit in the front with Mum on the drive to the new house and I was so excited. My brother Bobby and my sister Ruth were teenagers and they helped with the move. Dad was coming straight from work and we all couldn't wait to see the new house. When we arrived and I was lifted down from the van, I remember running into the house and being surprised at how big it was.

I was used to living in a bungalow and this new place had stairs. Everywhere was big to me and I was excited because it was ours. After the unloading was done, my brother helped mum set the beds up and my sister began to unpack the essentials. We discovered the electric hadn't yet been turned on, but we had a big open fireplace and that was the next job, lighting the fire. As it got dark, we lit candles and Mum made beans on toast on the fire. When dad came in from work, we had our first meal in our new house, and it felt good. Bobby got a room of his own because he was the only boy and Ruth and I shared a bigger room. A new life in a new place had begun, and everyone was happy.

The outside of the house had to have the ground dug to prepare for the gardens. I remember my grandad with his spade beginning to dig out the hard ground for soil to be put down. At four years old, I wanted to help. Mum took me to a toy shop and bought me a gardening set complete with a wheelbarrow, and grandad gave me my patch of ground to dig. I didn't make a lot of progress with my plastic spade though. Eventually grass seed was planted and we had a proper garden. In September that year I began school. I didn't like changes as a child. I'd have been happy to stay home with Mum but off I went to begin my education. The best time was when the bell rang for home time though.

One day a minister knocked at the front door and Mum invited him in. He was the Reverend Hartley, a tall man with grey hair and a nice smile. He sat down and chatted and invited Mum to the Methodist Church on the Springfield Road. On Sunday morning she and I went to church and I loved it. There was also a Sunday School and a choir and later, when I was old enough, I joined the Girls Brigade and the youth club. I was happy as a child and I got to meet new friends.

I loved to sing so the choir was my favourite and then when I was older and joined the youth club, I used to sing on a Saturday night. I loved being on the stage and I had dreams of being a singer when I grew up.

My Sunday School teacher was a nurse, so my dreams expanded, and I was going to be a nurse as well. I smile when I think back to that time. So many ambitions and an excitement of all the things I wanted to do in my life.

We stayed in the Methodist Church for several years. This part of my life is so significant because I was spiritually aware of God. He wasn't just someone the minister talked about on Sunday. I knew there was more to it. I got a prize at the yearly Sunday School party and it was called, 101 Best Bible Stories. I began to read it and couldn't put it down.

I knew that Jesus was a real person and not a story book character and I began to change inside, and I began to pray. When the time came to do my exam for the Girls Brigade there was a written page to do. The last question was for me to write out Matthew 28:18-20, the Great Commission that Jesus gave to the disciples. I had spent weeks learning it and when I saw the question on the page, I knew I could do this.

Afterwards I was walking up home, and I was so happy because it felt like Jesus was walking beside me. I knew I'd got the verses right for my exam and I was so thankful he had helped me. I was happier when I got my badge for passing the exam.

Childlike faith is innocent and precious, it is trusting and having that connection with Jesus is the safest place for me to be.

Mark 10:14-16

'Let the children come to me. Don't stop them! For the Kingdom of God belongs to those who are like these children. I tell you the truth, anyone who doesn't receive the Kingdom of God like a child will never enter it.' Then

he (Jesus) took the children in his arms and placed his hands on their heads and blessed them.

Being a child of God doesn't mean remaining childish, but childlike in faith. I experience that childlike faith when I talk to my Father, I live it in my daily life and when I need that reassurance in moments of stress, then I pray, 'Lord I need you.'

God is in control of my life, but it wasn't always that way. It took many years for me to surrender my heart and my will to him. He is so patient, and his grace gently wooed me to him. But, more about that later.

When I was ten, my young sister Sharon was born and she was tiny, all three pounds of her. I had dolls bigger than her. She was in the hospital for a few weeks until she gained weight and when she came home, I couldn't wait to take her out in the pram. She was a novelty until she cried and then I gave her back to Mum. She was tiny and cute, and she was my baby sister. Sometimes though I forgot we had her. One day Mum asked me to go down the road to the local Co-op for a few things and I wanted to take Sharon in the pram. So, I set off, aged ten, but feeling like a grown up. I had my shopping bag with the purse and shopping list in the pram. I got to the shop and felt proud of myself getting the groceries and putting the change back into the purse. I set off home again feeling happy until I was halfway up the road and realised something was missing. Yes, I'd left Sharon outside the Co-op. I ran so fast down the road, I was praying out loud, 'Please God don't let anyone steal my sister.' When I got back to the shop, Sharon had woken up from her sleep and a passer-by was smiling into the pram at the lovely baby. I began to walk back up home and I was nearly in tears. I kept saying sorry to the baby, as if she would know but I was so frightened by what could have happened. When I got home, I told my Mum what I did and she laughed, she said I was a silly girl but sure everyone was ok. It took a lot more out of me than it did Sharon or Mum. I felt so responsible even though I was only ten. I was a lot more careful in the future!

My Mum and I loved to go to the Christian book shops in Belfast as both of us loved books. I also got stickers and colouring in books. We spent a lot of time over the years in the book shops. It was our hobby.

I remember reading in a story that one day Jesus was coming back to earth and of course I thought it could be anytime. I used to come out of school and wonder if he would be at the school gates waiting for me. My imagination knew no bounds and as my childish faith grew so did my awareness of God as my Father, and I was his child.

My Mum became ill after Sharon was born and we now recognise postnatal depression as a serious illness. I was too young to understand depression, I was ten. I did know that mum didn't feel well enough to go to the book shops again and she wasn't happy. She didn't go to church much anymore and at times I felt lonely, my security as I'd known it was slipping away and I didn't understand why. My mum saw the doctor and was given treatment. I was told to be a good girl as Mum needed to rest. There were other changes at home that I was finding hard to cope with.

My brother Bobby had gotten married and moved out. He used to work night shift back then and I remember going to stay with my sister-in-law Jeannie. There was an ice cream shop across the road where they lived, and we used to go over and buy treats before bed. I loved that.

My sister Ruth got married the year after and she and her husband Fred lived at my parents' house.

At that time Sharon was a baby and my elder sister Ruth helped to look after her. I was aware of the changes at home and I retreated into my quiet self, reading my books and being a good girl. I was in primary five in school and I remember sharing with my teacher that I had a new baby sister. At home, I liked to get away to my room and sit on the bed and read. This had always been my happy place, or on a sunny day I would put a big blanket out in the back garden and read. I didn't want to be bothered with whatever was going on.

With Mum being ill and my sister running the house with the help of her husband Fred, I kind of got forgotten about. I was happy in my room with my books and I was also out of everyone's way.

One day in school the nurse came in to check everyone's head for lice. It didn't bother me as she came in every year and looked in your head and said all was fine. I lined up with everyone else and she looked in my hair which was long. On the way out at lunchtime the teacher called me to one side and put a pink card in my hand and said I should give it to my Mum. I didn't know what it meant but some of the other kids did. I got home and gave her card to Mum and immediately she began looking in my hair and I had lice and nits and I heard her say, my head was walking off me. Well in my imagination I got a picture of my head walking off with its own legs and of course I thought it was funny, apparently not! I had to have this smelly treatment and my hair combed through with a fine metal toothed comb and it was sore. They put a newspaper on the living room floor, and I knelt over it and honestly, there was a whole world hibernating in my head. Eventually I got my hair cut short but I was aware other kids stayed away from me in school and for the first time in my life I knew what it was like to be different, I felt dirty and embarrassed and I'd never had that feeling before. It stayed with me for a long time.

There was a lot of tension at home and sometimes Mum and Dad kicked off with each other. I didn't like shouting and I used to tell them to stop. One night after a huge row mum decided she had had enough; I remember her saying it, but I didn't know what enough was. She put Sharon in the high pram and put my coat on and we went out for a walk. It was still winter because it was dark and cold. We walked for a long time down the Springfield Road and she didn't say a lot except to assure me that everything would be alright. Further down the road she stopped with the pram and looked back up the road and then she told me I should go back home to daddy and that she would get a place for her and Sharon and she would come and get me. Now at age ten I knew nothing about having a gut feeling, but I knew that if I left her, I wouldn't see her again. The feeling inside me was so strong because I knew in my heart if she walked away from me, I would lose her and Sharon. Everything inside me was shouting for me not to walk back up that dark road, I had to stay with Mum, I couldn't leave her.

So, I told her I was going nowhere, besides, I was frightened to walk back up the road on my own. Eventually she turned the pram and said we would both go home. I felt so relieved. I honestly don't know what mum would have done if I had left her but thankfully, I didn't have to find out.

Eventually Mum began to get better and one Sunday night she decided we were going to a gospel meeting that was being held in a tent. I was puzzled, I'd never been to a meeting in a tent and I wondered why they didn't have a hall. Off we went, Mum, Dad, me and baby Sharon. Mum loved the meeting, and we went back again and then some people came to the house and explained the bible more to us. I got to go to the kid's holiday bible school, and I loved it. My parents decided to join the church and of course, I was going too. We got baptised and we began to go to church. Our home was good again and I was happy.

I loved church on a Sunday morning because now I could take Communion. I felt like a real Christian and I imagined my life would always feel happy and good.

From age ten until thirteen I enjoyed what I had. I loved when we came home from church and sat down for dinner at the table and Sharon was in her highchair and Dad would say grace and we would hold hands. I loved that feeling of belonging in a family. Dad used to sing at open air meetings, and I used to sing with him as I was learning harmony then, when I was eleven singing with my Dad felt good. However, when he still wanted me to do it at thirteen, I wouldn't, well it wasn't cool then to sing with your Dad.

I enjoyed my young life until I hit the teenage years and then I began to change. My sweet and innocent personality soon turned to rebellion as I discovered a different side to life. I had been involved in every activity in church and I was never in any kind of trouble. I lived in my own wee bubble. When I became a teenager and discovered pop music in 1968/69, I loved it. I knew every song in the charts. I preferred pop music to singing hymns. I also discovered make-up and I was quick at learning how to do eye make-up, foundation and lipstick and I was in class with the eye liner! Unfortunately, it didn't go down well in church or with my dad. It was here I hit my rebellion stage.

My Dad was a quiet man, hardworking providing for his family but strict. He worried because he cared. I was a teenager; I didn't see him that way. I thought he was spoiling my fun. 1969 was the hippy era and I just wanted to be a hippy and go to San Francisco. I loved mini dresses and I had long hair that I could back comb and I'd put glittery stars on my cheeks and a beauty spot. I'd make my entrance into the living room and Dad would look up from behind the newspaper and say, 'Are you going out like that?' We did argue sometimes although Mum didn't seem to mind.

I was a teenager, and my Dad didn't like the changes. I was also outspoken even though I knew I'd get in trouble, I had to say my piece. For a few years Dad and I butted heads although I still went to church, I did lighten the make-up for church though, keeping Dad happy was high on my agenda. I also left school in 1969, which I was glad to see the back of because I wanted to work and earn money and be able to buy things.

By the time I was fifteen the dynamics at home had changed. Mum had been ill on and off since Sharon was born with postnatal depression. She could be well for a long time and then she would get depressed and she struggled with life. It was a sad time because she didn't go to church often and the days of her and I going to the book shops were over. It was a confusing time for me because I remember what it used to be like when we were a family at the dinner table and dad said grace. That didn't happen now either. I was still into music, make-up and now boys. I had a few teenage crushes and I smile as I think back to those days. By the time I turned sixteen I'd met the man I would marry. He was older than me and that didn't go down well with dad, but he accepted it because we went to church.

As I got older the innocence of my childhood faith seemed to have disappeared and I knew more about religion and living right. For example, if I stopped wearing makeup and dressed in longer dresses as opposed to short ones, someone would take notice and it would have been seen as an improvement. No one ever talked to me about my heart towards God, being a Christian became a set of rules and sometimes I broke the rules. I wanted to be a Christian, but I also wanted to be free to be myself. I think I might have been ahead of my time. There was something lacking in me and I looked to find the answer in church, yet I wasn't finding it there. I could keep all the rules, but I only had to break one and I felt so bad about myself. It was like walking a tightrope and it would only be a matter of time before I got it all wrong. I used to think I wasn't good enough for God to love me. My rebellion with authority came to a head one Sunday afternoon. I'd been to church that morning and I had enjoyed it. I was feeling happy as I waited around after church talking to people. It was a lovely sunny day and I went to tell my dad I was going to walk on home. As I turned the sun caught the glitter in my blue eyeshadow and a member of the church leadership remarked that Delilah painted her eyes, I laughed and said she wasn't as good as me. I went home and forgot about the remark; it had been said in fun, so I never gave it a second thought.

Dad came home later than usual and when he came in, I knew that something was wrong with him. He came straight at me and demanded my makeup bag and began throwing stuff in the fire. I wasn't having any of it. I took it off him and asked him what was wrong. Apparently, someone in church had a word with him about me and he didn't like it. My make-up wasn't what they thought I should be wearing to church. Dad thought people were talking behind his back about his daughter and he was angry that someone in leadership had taken him aside to have a word with him.

What followed was a full-scale war between him and I. He wanted to burn my makeup and I wasn't letting it go. He got angry and lost control and I got hurt. I still wouldn't give in, though. That afternoon I sat up in my room, I was grounded as well. The worst thing about it though was that I had really enjoyed church that morning, I was happy walking down home and there was no way I could foresee what was about to kick off. Something inside me began to shut down that day. I was sad but I had to let it happen. I'd had enough of living by rules and being told to be good and don't cause any trouble. No one talked about the love of Jesus, yet people watched to see who wasn't doing things right. Dad hurt me that day and both of us said a lot of angry words to each other. I'd had enough and decided to finish with church. I didn't need that pressure. I felt rejected by my dad and by others, I didn't feel good enough. I hid the hurt in my heart and worst of all, I felt I'd never be good enough for God and that just proved to me that I could never be a Christian so I made myself a promise that I would guard my heart from getting hurt like that again. Eventually dad and I made peace, he knew he had lost control and he knew it shouldn't have happened.

Dad wasn't one to say sorry, but he had his own way of doing things. One day he came home from work and he had a big bag for me. I opened it and in it were two coats. My dad had good taste and he told me to pick one. He worked next to a fashion warehouse and he knew some of the staff there. I chose a lovely ivory coat with gold buttons; it was beautiful, and I loved it. Accepting the coat from him was our way of being friends again. Peace reigned between dad and I for another while, but I stayed away from church. I'd put a boundary line in place, and I'd closed my heart to church. I still believed everything about God, but I didn't feel good enough for church. I prayed and read books and my bible, but I needed to feel safe and being in church meant being vulnerable and I wasn't going down that path again. What I didn't realise in my spiritual immaturity was that I had an enemy who was out to rob, steal and destroy my life, he would kill if he could. The seeds of resentment being sown in my heart and the rejection that I kept hidden would eventually bear fruit and the harvest wouldn't be pretty. Slowly, over time I began to view God like I viewed my dad. If I was good then things would be fine but when something hurt me emotionally because I felt I'd broken his rules then I saw God as the one with the big stick and when I stepped out of line then I was in trouble. The rebel in me continued to push the boundaries and I remember the first time I drank sparkling wine; two drinks and I was gone! At seventeen I felt I was grown up and all that had gone before became a distant memory. I thought I knew so much yet I knew nothing. I was hurting inside, and God was hurting for me, but it would take a few years before that revelation dawned. I had bigger plans. I got married at seventeen, my dad had to give his consent which he did, I think he was glad of some peace and quiet when I moved out. Life was by no means wonderful, but I was making the best of it, or maybe a bigger mess of it.

At times I would open my bible, but it was just words on a page. No longer did I feel the excitement I once had and again I got the thought that I would never be good enough to be a Christian. I felt sad inside sometimes and I was sorry life had turned out the way it had. I missed church too, but I just couldn't go there again. I couldn't risk being hurt again. I was sinking to a new depth in life, I'd chosen to make my decisions and be the one in control. I'd put God on the back burner yet somewhere deep inside of me I knew he was still there; I just wasn't ready to face him just yet. Having spent so many years in church, many of which I enjoyed, I noticed the changes as soon as I left.

I felt under less pressure, I had my freedom, and no one was going to tell me what to do. I was making my own decisions because now I was a grown up. Oh my, the deception I began to live under. Yes, I had turned my back on religion, and I thought I could plan out the rest of my life my way and the sense of freedom that gave me was thrilling. I didn't realise then that once you are a child of God you never stop being his child, something I'm forever thankful for. At this stage in my life I thought I could turn my back and that would be it, obviously I had some lessons to learn!

Chapter 2

My husband and I got married in 1971 and I loved my wedding day. My dress was lovely with lace and chiffon sleeves and the lace coat fastened with pearl buttons on a little gold chain. We got married in the registry office in College Street, Belfast and on the way there the police stopped our car as there was a bomb scare on route. When they saw me in my wedding dress, we got a police escort to the registry office. The joys of living in Belfast! I enjoyed being married, we were young and in love and the world seemed a rosier place. Then real-life kicks in and like all marriages we had our share of hard times. The good times were good there just wasn't enough of them.

We were married three years when I discovered a lump on my breast. I was sitting in my chair knitting and we had a cat that used to sit on my shoulders. I felt my bra strap slide down and I put my hand down to fix it. As my hand passed over my breast, I felt the lump. I went up to the bathroom for a closer look and I could feel it. Fear was the first thing that went through me. I was twenty years old and I wanted children and if this was cancer then maybe that would never happen. I told my husband and he tried to console me but first thing the next morning I was at the doctors.

I was referred to the Royal Hospital and I got an appointment quickly. When I saw the consultant, he examined me and thought the lump was nothing to worry about. It was probably an abscess and he could drain it. I was still worried that it was cancer, but I was told a tumour was a more solid lump. He did the biopsy, but the needle didn't drain the lump, it stuck in it and I was so scared as it took the help of another doctor to get it out. I was told I would need surgery as soon as possible.

I went home more worried than ever and went back to work the next morning. Two weeks before Christmas I came home from work and there was a telegram in the hall from the hospital. This was in the days when email didn't exist. I was to be admitted a few days later for surgery. I didn't know whether to be relieved or more worried. It was happening quicker than I thought.

In 1974 there were no mammograms or scans of any kind. The night before my operation a nurse was talking me through the procedure, and I was asked to sign a consent form for a mastectomy, and I was shocked. I was twenty years old and I felt frightened signing the form. She explained that while I was asleep, a sample of tissue would be examined and if the tumour was malignant then they would perform a mastectomy but if it was benign, they would remove it and stitch up the wound. Going into the theatre the next morning my fear was that I wouldn't know anything until it was over, and I was so nervous. I prayed that things would go well and despite my backslidden heart I knew God still heard me

I woke up in recovery, in pain, and a thick bandage covered me. I immediately thought that my breast had been removed and I was upset. A lovely nurse came over to me and through my tears I said, 'Is there one or two?' She laughed and assured me there were two and the tumour was benign, so they removed a lump and an abscess, and I was going to be fine. I got an injection for pain and drifted into a lovely sleep. I was allowed home a few days later and told to come back on the day after Boxing day to get my stitches out. The crisis was over, and I was able to recover at home.

Once the stitches came out, I was left with a scar which I still have but I know it could have been so different and I was thankful to God that I was well. I recovered and went back to work.

Having the scare with cancer changed the way I felt about having children. I always knew I wanted them, but we had been in no hurry. We decided it was time and in 1975 we had good news, I was pregnant with our first child and in November our baby girl was born. We named her Julie Ann and I was so happy to be a mum. We had our second child, a son, Paul in 1978 and I was happy being a mum of two. My mum bought me a Silver Cross high pram and I loved that pram. On a sunny day I would be out walking with the sun canopy up, I could just about see over the top of it though.

I became an Avon representative to earn a bit of extra money and I used to deliver orders around my area. I had the baby in the pram, my daughter sitting on top and the orders on the shopping tray underneath. Everyone knew the Avon woman with the high pram. While I was happy being a mum, my marriage had problems and life was difficult. In 1978 we went to live in England for a fresh start but after a few months it just wasn't working so I brought the children back to Belfast and we moved in with my parents.

This was an incredibly sad time for me, and I struggled with depression. I was on treatment and I withdrew into myself. On the outside I was my usual smiley self but inside I thought I was dying. I felt so alone and the easiest way to handle it was to drink. I could be the life and soul of the party and I loved to dance. At times I would look in the mirror and I didn't recognise myself. All my dreams had turned into one big mess with no way out. In that black hole of depression I'd thought of taking my own life, I actually saw the benefit of me not being here anymore, no more pain, no more feeling I was a mess and yet the one thing that kept me going was my two children. I loved them more than life and they were the reason I got up out of bed in the morning. I thank God for them, they were my greatest gift and to this day they still are.

Despite being away from church for quite a few years, I still prayed and hoped for a better life. I was aware of the emptiness inside me that no tablets or alcohol would fill yet I didn't know what to do about it. I got through my day looking after my children and looked forward to a drink when they went to bed. I couldn't see any further than one day and I was stuck in a place in life that I didn't know how to get out of. I was lonely inside, but it wasn't for people, yet I didn't know what the answers were. At times I thought I would go crazy trying to find answers when I wasn't sure what the questions were! So, life continued in an existence and I went with the flow, yet I knew that there had to be more to life than this.

Somewhere deep inside me I was looking for a connection, yet anything I tried in life came up empty. I'd had jobs, a marriage and children but there was something missing. Deep down there was an emptiness and I didn't know what the solution was. I didn't really understand why I couldn't just have a normal life. I didn't realise at this time that while I had let go of God and church. God hadn't let go of me. That emptiness inside me was there because only a relationship with God would fill it and while I was doing life my way, there was a lack of connection. It is a spiritual thirst that exists within every human being and nothing in this world will fill that void. God made me body, soul and spirit and only he would be able to complete me. I felt that the loneliness I experienced inside was a spiritual one, but I really didn't see that at the time. I had this idea that being a good person and taking care of my children would give me the satisfaction I was looking for.

John 8:32 'And you will know the truth and the truth will set you free.'

What truth was I searching for? I would soon discover the meaning of my real identity

Chapter 3

The year 1979 brought about changes in me yet I couldn't understand what exactly was changing. I was twenty-five in May and I remember waking up on the morning of my birthday and knowing that something different was going to happen in my life. I was struggling with depression, drinking too much and feeling a total failure yet deep inside something felt different.

The summer that year was beautiful, and the children played out in the garden every day. My daughter had a little shopping trolley with packets of food, and she would set up her shop. My son Paul had started to walk and every chance he got he would take the trolley and run down the path with it laughing. They were happy and they gave me purpose for each day. Although I still struggled with depression, it was like shafts of sunlight were beginning to break through and for a short time I would feel so much better. Until the darkness came again.

Life continued in its usual vein, but I was aware of new hope inside me. I didn't understand why I felt hopeful, I just knew I did, and it was real. One summer night, a group of youth workers from a local church had a children's meeting near our house.

My children wanted to go so I walked up the street with them and they joined in. They sang songs and clapped their hands and heard a story. When it was over, they came away with a picture card with a bible verse and sweets and I smiled at their innocence, remembering my own. I began to wonder if what I'd experienced as a child had been real.

Those times when I had prayed, when I'd felt close to Jesus like he was my best friend. I was so happy then. Yet, at sixteen I had walked away, I remember thinking that I had outgrew God. I not only walked away from church but in my heart, I'd separated from him. I was a big girl then and all I wanted was to get married and have children and a home of my own. I saw a world that I wanted to experience, and I saw church as a place of religious rules, being nicely dressed and being a good person and the truth about me was that I couldn't live up to that. Well I had experienced the world that I thought was going to be so different and it was a deception. I discovered pain in all areas of life and finally the rose-tinted glasses came off. One night I couldn't sleep, and I borrowed a bible from my sister Sharon, it was one she had got as a Sunday school prize years before. I began to thumb through the scriptures I used to know, and I felt sad when I remembered how alive the bible used to be for me. I had closed myself down and I didn't know if I would ever find my way back. Maybe I would have to accept the decisions I'd made and get on with making the best of the life I now had. My greatest blessing was my children and I owed it to them to keep going. When I thought of all the nice people who went to church, I thought that there are some who seem to get it right and then there was me!

My struggle continued in the coming weeks although I did keep reading the bible when everyone was asleep. However, it was still just words, and I got little comfort from it. Now I was getting more confused. I had grown up to know God, been in church for years and walked away from it all. and now I struggled with the question, was there a way back for me?

My circumstances were still the same and the children were too young for me to go out to work, besides my parents both worked, and we lived in their house. So, from a practical perspective I was stuck. Mentally I had days that were better, and I had days when I would wake up and there was a brick wall in my mind, and it wouldn't come down. I saw that I was standing on the outside of my life looking in and I was trapped, combined with the spiritual struggle I had going on this was torment to my soul. It came to a head for me one night when I couldn't sleep.

I came downstairs and made a cup of tea and I thought of all the plans that had ended in disaster and I wanted to take myself away from the situation, away from life, A sense of hopelessness enveloped me and I began to think the children would be better off without me, maybe if I wasn't here then their lives would somehow be better. I thought of writing my parents a letter, and one for my children. The more I thought about it the more sensible it became. They say the darkest hour is just before dawn and until dawn broke, I battled the urge to end it all. I prayed; God help me. As I prayed, I saw a picture of my children playing in the garden, laughing and I saw myself hug them both and I realised I loved them more than life itself. I couldn't rob them of their mum or me of my life with them. I cried for a long time and it was daylight when I went to bed and slept. I was exhausted mentally and emotionally yet I knew that something deep had happened to me that night and there would be a turning point.

I felt calmer in the weeks ahead although I struggled with thoughts of having blown my chances and walked away. I had written myself off, but I was forgetting one important fact, God already knew all about me and he never gives up on his children. One weekend I was out with my family at a social event and during the evening I went to the ladies, as you do. I was happy, I'd had a few drinks and I was relaxed. Washing my hands, I glanced in the mirror, smiling at myself, when suddenly I felt hollow inside. I was puzzled. I'd been having a lovely evening yet, that one glance in the mirror told me something different. The real me was hollow and empty inside.

There was something missing in me and I didn't know what to do about it. There was a longing inside me and a deeper need that I couldn't fill myself.

I went back out to our table and continued smiling and talking yet deep inside I knew I wouldn't be back to this place; I didn't belong here. This wasn't the life I should be living, and it didn't matter how many drinks I would have, I would still feel empty. I was glad to get home and go to bed. I tried to read but it meant nothing, and I had a restless night. I knew my life had to change but I didn't know how to make any changes.

The next morning my parents went to work, and I tried to motivate myself for the day ahead. The children needed to be fed, washed and dressed and on Monday I did the laundry. Once the children were sorted and playing in the garden, I made a cup of tea and had a cigarette, this was my usual breakfast. I felt distressed inside. I replayed the night before and remembered that hollow feeling. I'd felt so empty. I was sinking to rock bottom and I struggled to accept the way my life had turned out. My desire for a better way of life had come to nothing and I didn't know how to change things. I was a single mum with two young children, living with my parents and I had a limited income. The reality of my life was nothing compared to the dreams I'd had of having a nice home and my children growing up in a family unit. I wanted better for my children and for myself, but I no longer had that motivation. I felt broken inside and emotionally I was battered. I didn't talk to anyone about how I felt as it was much easier to keep things in. I didn't know the direction my life was taking so there was no way that I could explain it to someone else.

Finally, I settled and began the housework and put the washing machine on, it was a twin tub, there were no automatics then. Once I had begun work, I enjoyed it and was fine if I kept focused. I love to see the washing on the clothesline outside in the sun. The children were playing in the garden and I called them in for a snack and I had a coffee.

My next job was the living room. Having two small children, there were usually toys and books lying around the room, so tidy up time was something I involved the children in although they found it funny and the toys never stayed in the toy box for too long. I was polishing the furniture in the living room and the children were running about playing and being noisy. I smiled as I listened to them laughing and I was thankful I had them. My mum had a writing bureau and on the top was a family bible, now no one ever read the bible, but it looked nice sitting there. I would dust the top of the bureau and put the bible back and I dusted it too. Lifting the bible down, it slipped, and I almost dropped it on the floor. I caught it quickly and as I went to close it, I glanced at the page it had fallen open at and I froze. It was like the words jumped off the page at me as I began to read.

'Thus, says the Lord, who created you, O Jacob and He who formed you, O Israel. Fear not, for I have redeemed you, I have called you by your name. You are Mine.' Isaiah 43:1

My heart was racing as I slammed the bible shut and put it back. I sat down on the chair and took a deep breath. 'God you have just spoken to me!' I lifted the bible and opened it and I read the verse again and again.

Deep inside, something in my spirit had ignited, and I felt a spark of life again. I sensed a connection for the first time in years. As the day went on, I told myself it was my imagination, why would God want to speak to me after all these years. I was the prodigal daughter yet there was no denying what I had read and how it had spoken to my heart.

My mind was clear and alert when I opened the bible and read it again, and it was life changing. Revelation began to dawn, God had said I was his, he had redeemed me, he had called me by my name. He knew my name!

That night I began to read in the bible about Moses. In Exodus chapter three Moses is out tending the sheep in the wilderness.

Exodus 3:1-15

One day Moses was tending the flock of his father-in-law, Jethro, the priest of Midian. He led the flock far into the wilderness and came to Sinai, the mountain of God. There the angel of the Lord appeared to him in a blazing fire from the middle of a bush. Moses stared in amazement. Though the bush was engulfed in flames, it didn't burn up. 'This is amazing,' Moses said to himself. 'Why isn't that bush burning up? I must go and see it.'

When the Lord saw Moses coming to take a closer look, God called to him from the middle of the bush, 'Moses! Moses!'

'Here I am.' Moses replied.

'Do not come any closer,' the Lord warned. 'Take off your sandals, for you are standing on holy ground. I am the God of Abraham, the God of Isaac, and the God of Jacob.'

When Moses heard this, he covered his face because he was afraid to look at God.

Then the Lord told him. 'I have certainly seen the oppression of my people in Egypt. I have heard their cries of distress because of their harsh slave drivers. Yes, I am aware of their suffering. So, I have come down to rescue them from the power of the Egyptians and lead them out of Egypt into their own fertile and spacious land. It is a land flowing with milk and honey – the place where the Canaanites, Hittites, Amorites, Perizzites, Hivites, and Jebusites now live. Look, the cry of the people of Israel has reached me, and I have seen how harshly the Egyptians abuse them. Now go, for I am sending you to Pharaoh. You must lead my people Israel out of Egypt. But Moses protested to God. 'Who am I to appear before Pharaoh? Who am I to lead the people of Israel out of Egypt?'

God answered. 'I will be with you. And this is your sign that I am the one who has sent you: When you have brought the people out of Egypt, you will worship God at this very mountain.'

But Moses protested. 'If I go to the people of Israel and tell them. 'The God of your ancestors has sent me to you.' They will ask me, 'What is his name?' Then what should I tell them?'

God replied to Moses. 'I AM WHO I AM. Say this to the people of Israel: Yahweh, the God of your ancestors – the God of Abraham, the God of Isaac, and the God of Jacob – has sent me to you. This is my eternal name. my name to remember for all generations.'

Now I love this passage of scripture because it's God and Moses having a conversation. God wants Moses to go to Egypt, but Moses had a few things to say about it. Yet God had chosen him, he had called Moses by name from the burning bush.

I thought back to that morning when God spoke to me and I had to smile. I wonder if Moses was as overwhelmed as I had been when the words of *Isaiah 43:1* had jumped off the page at me. God seems to like surprising people!

Now Moses had been living in the land of Midian having ran away from Egypt forty years before. Yet God hadn't forgotten about him and in his timing, he called Moses and Moses knew who he was. I too had run away from God, the rebellious teenager who was going to conquer the world, but God hadn't forgotten about me either. I'm thankful it didn't take forty years though! When he spoke to me and told me, '…I have called you by name; you are mine.' I knew in my spirit that I had heard his voice.

When I read the bible, the words came alive again, just like they had years before. I was excited at the possibility of a new beginning and then I'd wonder if I had got it wrong, maybe I was really setting myself up for a fall. I struggled to discern between what my emotions were shouting at me and believing what I had read in the bible. I believed the word of God to be true so now I had to apply it to myself. I believe God had thrown me a lifeline and I was holding on tight.

My struggle with God went on for several weeks until I felt emotionally exhausted and spiritually thirsty. At times when I read my bible, I got comfort and hope from the scriptures, then I would remember all my failures and I was back in that place of not being good enough. One morning

I was reading the gospel of Luke and it tells of Jesus being invited to the house of Simon the Pharisee for dinner.

Luke 7:36

'One of the Pharisees asked Jesus to have dinner with him, so Jesus went to his home and sat down to eat. When a certain immoral woman from that city heard he was eating there, she brought a beautiful alabaster jar filled with expensive perfume. Then she knelt behind his feet, weeping. Her tears fell on his feet, and she wiped them off with her hair. Then she kept kissing his feet and putting perfume on them. When the Pharisee who had invited him saw this, he said to himself, 'If this man were a prophet, he would know what kind of woman is touching him. She's a sinner!' Then Jesus answered his thoughts. 'Simon,' he said to the Pharisee, 'I have something to say to you.'

'Go ahead teacher,' Simon replied.

Then Jesus told him a story. 'A man loaned money to two people- 500 pieces of silver to one and 50 pieces to the other. But neither of them could repay him, so he kindly forgave them both, cancelling their debts. Who do you suppose loved him more after that?'

Simon answered. 'I suppose the one for whom he cancelled the larger debt.'

'That's right,' Jesus said. Then he turned to the woman and said to Simon. 'Look at this woman kneeling here. When I entered your home, you didn't offer me water to wash the dust from my feet, but she washed them with her tears and wiped them with her hair. You didn't greet me with a kiss but from the time I first came in, she has not stopped kissing my feet. You neglected the courtesy of olive oil to anoint my head, yet she has anointed my feet with rare perfume. I tell

you, her sins – and they are many – have been forgiven, so she has shown me much love. Then Jesus looked at the woman. 'Your sins are forgiven.'

The men at the table said among themselves, 'Who is this man, that he goes around forgiving sins?'

And Jesus said to the woman. 'Your faith has saved you; go in peace.'

The woman left the house a different person to the one who had arrived. Jesus had given her a new beginning in life. He gave her acceptance without expecting anything else from her and I think it is beautiful that the scriptures don't name the woman, Jesus gave her back her dignity. How amazing that her every need was met as her heart connected with the one who loved her the most. She was broken when she came to him and cried her tears as she poured perfume on his feet, and she found in him cleansing from sin and acceptance instead of scorn.

Jesus referred to her faith, all she had she gave to him and he gave her what she needed most. Forgiveness, love and hope. She received the miracle she needed, and she went away complete.

In reading this I felt the same as this woman, I'd made lots of mistakes and didn't feel good enough to come back to him, yet, here he is saying that it isn't about feeling good enough, he accepts me as I am and welcomes me.

So many times, in the past I had remembered the faith I'd had as a child and I missed it but believing I was a failure and not good enough always had been a hindrance to me. I desired to have that faith again, but I felt I'd blown my relationship with God and I didn't know the way back. I struggled for a while, comparing myself to others and of course, in my eyes, everyone was better than me. More restless nights followed. Now the Lord knows that I like my sleep, but I couldn't settle. I was still restless, and it took some time for me to realise that I couldn't fix myself, I needed God.

Finally, I decided I couldn't argue with him any longer. I had to stop hiding from him and be honest. Alone in my bedroom I began to pray. I was thankful for the word that God had given me in *Isaiah 43:1*, but then I began to tell him all the reasons why he should stay out of my life. I reminded him that I'd failed him before, and I know I had hurt him and probably would again. Whatever he wanted with me, I thought it might be better if he talked to someone else. I reminded him of all my sins and while I believed I was forgiven did he really want to take a chance on me again? When I ran out of excuses I sat down on the bed and cried. I felt so lonely inside and yet I knew in my heart that God loved me. So why was I so scared? Maybe he would expect too much of me and I would fail or maybe I would expect too much of myself and failing might just damage me further. I sat quietly and I sensed the silence in my spirit, like God was waiting for me to respond. I could struggle through life, doing it my way or I could surrender to God and have a new beginning.

I knew I was at that point where I could step forward into something new or I could stay stuck and struggle. I knew he was drawing me towards him, yet, I had been shrinking back. Taking a deep breath, I began to pray. I asked him to take me back and I promised never to go away again.

Suddenly it was like coming home and I wept as I found love and acceptance with him. I'd stepped across a boundary into the arms of my Father where I belonged. I was so sorry it had taken so long. It felt like a huge weight lifted off me and I experienced real freedom. I don't remember how long I stayed in that place with him but the peace that flooded my being was healing and pure joy. I knew now that whatever happened in life, I would never have to face it alone. I was truly back to where I belonged. I walked out of my room that day a different person and I had confidence in my spirit that had been lacking for so many years. Jesus Christ is the rock-solid foundation that my life is built upon, the Son of God died to save me and give me a new life and I said, 'yes Lord.'

Looking back on my years when I'd kept God in the background of my life and church was almost a bad word, I was blown away at how deceived I'd become. When I first walked away from him, I experienced a feeling of freedom and my life being my own, that was before I messed it up. Making mistakes wasn't a big failure because everyone makes mistakes and gets into messes. My failure was deceiving myself into thinking that a life without God was going to be so much better, but I hadn't reckoned on the loneliness of my spirit that would eventually affect me mentally, emotionally and even physically. During my years in church I had become religious and had tried to live by the rules. My revelation had shown me that real life isn't about religion, it's about relationships. I now had something a lot more precious, I had a relationship with God, I was up close and personal with the one who loves me the most. All those years of wandering through life and he waited until I was at the end of myself, until I was thirsty for him again and my soul hungered for the one who is the bread of life. God never gave up on me, but I'd given up on myself.

He waited until my rebellion had worn me out and I realised that it wasn't the church or religion I was rebelling against, but it was him. His grace began to draw me back to him, slowly, because I was so fragile and broken. His grace produced within me the hunger and thirst for him because no one or nothing can satisfy my soul like he does. He waited patiently until I cried out to him and then he brought me to himself. God never gives up on his children, no matter the circumstances, he is waiting. There is always a new beginning with him and there is nothing that I could ever do that would make him love me less. So, what's so amazing about grace, well it's amazing.

When I think back to the story of Cinderella and how the Prince found her, I smile at her happy ending. For me, my Prince of Peace, Jesus, found me and drew me to him. I don't live in a happily ever after fairy tale, but in a life where I experience a real relationship with the Prince who gave his very life for me, out of his great love I found life.

Ephesians 2:8-10

'God saved you by his grace when you believed. And you can't take credit for this; it is a gift from God. Salvation is not a reward for the good things we have done, so none of us can boast about it. For we are God's masterpiece. He has created us anew in Christ Jesus, so we can do the good things he planned for us long ago.'

For so many years I had felt in a desert place where it was empty of love and relationship and it was dry. My soul longed to be quenched, yet I continued to wander. The desert in my soul was lonely and without purpose. It felt like my life was being slowly suffocated by pressure in my mind. There was a part of me crying out for change and knowing that God was the answer but there is also an enemy who was quick to remind me of my failures and the reasons I had walked away many years before. The bible says that we are not to give place to the devil. Well, I brought him in and made him a cup of tea!

It seems to be so much easier to listen to the lies of the enemy because it will all be negative and when I wasn't feeling good about myself anyway, his lies almost made sense! Except, I was still God's child and it didn't matter if I knew it or felt or even believed it. God hadn't let me go, I walked away but now he was bringing me back into a relationship with him.

The greatest loneliness is a spiritual one. It is in a place where you cry deeply and only the love of God can fill that void. When I surrendered my heart to him, I was accepted, loved and welcomed into his arms. In worshipping God, I experience that beautiful love that embraces my soul. This is real life and nothing else can satisfy a soul or quench the spirit like the love of Christ. New beginnings start deep inside with the Creator who made me. Connecting with him changed my perspective on life as I realised, I was loved. I'd thought I wasn't good enough and that lie of the enemy had held me back for a long time. Now I knew that because Jesus died and shed his blood for me, I was worthy to be called a child of God. He paid the price for my sin and through him I have life and relationship with my Father. It took a long time for me to realise that I am body, soul and spirit and to try and live my life without all these areas being fulfilled was foolish. God made me and he fulfils every area of my life and nothing or no one else can do that. It begins with him and my relationship grows with him.

Ephesians 2:10

For we are God's masterpiece. He has created us anew in Christ Jesus, so we can do the good things he planned for us long ago.'

Chapter 4

Every morning I awoke, I was aware of a new beginning in my life. The assurance that I was in a relationship with the Lord gave me a foundation on which my life was now built. Whatever happened now or in the future I knew I had him to lean on, to trust and to talk to. I loved my bible, I loved to sing, and worship and I loved the peace of heart and mind that he had given to me. His love is real and at times I wondered why did it take so long for me to return to him? My desire to do life my way had resulted in pride and rebellion and that sin separated me from God. Yet, when I said yes to him, I received his forgiveness and I felt so new and clean and peace flooded my being.

I loved going to church and my children went to Sunday school. I felt a giant weight had been lifted off my life although that didn't mean my life was problem free. The one area of my life that caused me pain was the end of my marriage. I was going through divorce proceedings and this was a traumatic time for me and my children. Every marriage has problems at some point and I always thought we would work things out. I never got married thinking that one day I would face divorce and it overwhelmed me. I had to accept that sometimes relationships don't work out and there is nowhere else to go with it except divorce.

The morning I went to court I was nervous, but the actual proceedings didn't take long. Afterwards I walked down the long corridor and sat down on a bench, I felt so empty inside. My marriage had just been dissolved and it was over. I felt a sense of failure and emotionally I was exhausted. Walking out of the court I stood in the fresh air for a few minutes and then took a deep breath. I had two children that I was responsible for now and today was a different beginning for us. I remembered a scripture I had been reading before I went to court that morning.

Isaiah 41:10

'Don't be afraid, for I am with you. Don't be discouraged for I am your God. I will strengthen you and help you. I will hold you up with my victorious right hand.'

At times I found coping with the changes difficult and I did hit a wall of depression after the divorce. It was like I was grieving inside and, in a way I was. Divorce brought home to me the death of a marriage and I did grieve. Whatever plans I thought we had for the future would never happen now and it was hard to accept. I worried about the children too, yet they were so adaptable. They were surrounded by family and I think that helped. I had a lot to be thankful for really. I now had a home, a job and a family supporting me so while the changes were difficult, at least we were surviving. Being a single parent carried a lot of responsibility and at times it was overwhelming. I felt lonely and I missed being part of a couple and having someone to share my life with. There was an emptiness inside, and it was a part of me that I hid away. No one would have known how I was feeling as I was good at smiling and behaving like everything was alright. The one thing that helped me through this was reading my bible. The more I read about different characters in the bible, I was able to draw closer to God and learn from what I was reading. I discovered the joy of finding scriptures that related to my circumstances and I was strengthened by what I read. The Lord was teaching me to trust him, he knew all about my life and my family and I had the assurance that he would never leave me.

Working five days a week gave me the weekend to look forward to. I used to come home from work on a Friday with the weekly shopping. After a cup of tea, I did the housework, put the washing on and then when I'd finished, I'd have a nice bath. I was tired when I went to bed, but it felt so good knowing the work was done. On a Saturday morning the children would be up watching television and I would stay in bed reading a book, having a cup of tea. I loved Saturdays. I enjoyed spending time in my room with my bible and a notebook. I would write down the things that God was speaking to my heart and I was drawn in a more intimate relationship with him. Deep in my spirit I was experiencing the depth of love God has for me, and it helped to heal me emotionally and strengthened me. Reading through the book of Isaiah I came to chapter 54 and it touched my very soul.

Isaiah 54:4-8

'Do not be afraid; you will not suffer shame. Do not fear disgrace; you will not be humiliated. You will forget the shame of your youth and remember no more the reproach of your widowhood. For your Maker is your husband- the Lord Almighty is his name- the Holy One of Israel is your Redeemer, he is called the God of all the earth. The Lord will call you back, as if you were a wife distressed in spirit- a wife who married young, only to be rejected, says your God. In a surge of anger, I hid my face from you for a moment, but with everlasting kindness I will have compassion on you, says the Lord your Redeemer.'

The verses in Isaiah were life changing for me. God was showing the depth of his love for me and in my spirit, I began to realise that he is indeed a husband and not just to me. Any woman on your own could relate to these scriptures, it doesn't matter if you are single, married, divorced or widowed, the God of all the earth is a husband to you. I am loved and the more time I spent reading and praying the more I saw my identity was in him.

The difficult times when I struggled in life was when I was surrounded by married couples, either at a social gathering or in church. I felt like the square peg in a round hole, but this was another challenge that I had to face up to, but I always did it with a smile. I was on my own for several years and I began to wonder if I would ever meet anyone special. I used to feel vulnerable being on my own and so I withdrew into myself and focussed on my family and my work and my home.

I loved buying books and that was my hobby. It was on a trip to the Faith Mission that I discovered books by Catherine Marshall. The first book I bought I was hooked. Catherine had been married to Peter Marshall, a Scottish minister. Peter died suddenly and Catherine found herself widowed with a young son and a small income. I had finally found someone I could really identify with. It was like finding a new friend. I bought every book Catherine had written and I was so encouraged by her relationship with God and how she learnt to handle new challenges in her life. She helped me so much.

Catherine also inspired my dream to be a writer, a dream I tended to bury because I thought it was just a dream. Yet, as I read about her life, I felt that prompting in my spirit that I was to dig up my dream and start to believe in it. I remember the first time I ever felt the desire to write was when I was a little girl. I was ill and I think it was measles, and my mum had made me a bed on the sofa in front of the open fire. I was aware I was ill, and when I wasn't sleeping,

I was reading. I was about eight or nine years old at the time and my dad came home from work one night and handed me a large brown envelope. When I opened it, I found pencils and pens and lots of yellow A4 paper. The staff in the office where he worked heard I was ill and sent them to me. I had never seen yellow A4 paper before and suddenly it was if a light was switched on inside me. I wanted to write so I announced to my parents that I was going to be a writer when I grew up. They smiled and humoured me, but I knew that I would write. A few months later I wrote my first poem and it was published in the church newsletter.

As an adult I would write for the church magazine and I was always writing short stories, although none of those got published! I kept writing because I loved to sit down with a pen and notebook and look at a blank page and want to fill it with words. It helped me to write and I believed that writing would be a big part of my life.

Catherine Marshall wrote her first book after she became a widow and was raising a young son herself. She had to learn to trust the Lord in a completely new way, not just for her needs but for how she felt about herself. I found that being married and having a husband was part of my identity but when circumstances changed, my status changed also, to that of divorced and that affected how I felt about myself. Like Catherine, I found a new learning curve with God, yet I was aware that there was still a gap in my life. In marriage I liked being a wife and having a husband but after the divorce there was a void inside, and I needed to depend on God more than ever.

One Christmas my mum bought me a book called, *The Christian's Secret of a Happy Life*, by Hannah Whittall Smith. I loved getting books at Christmas and having an early night with some chocolate and a cup of tea, I began to read through the book. I was really enjoying it until I came to chapter twelve. It was called, 'Is God in Everything?' As I read it, I found I had a problem with it.

I'd just come through a painful divorce, gone back to full time work and had my life turned upside down and I'll be honest, there were times I found it hard to accept that God was in everything. I knew my scriptures though.

1 Thessalonians 5:16-18.

'Be joyful always; pray continually; give thanks in all circumstances, for this is God's will for you in Christ Jesus.'

It is sometimes hard to find God in difficult circumstances, yet when I do, I find peace. Getting to that point is a different matter! I'd read so many scriptures and agreed with them yet inside me there was that little word. 'But.' It's easy to find God in pleasant circumstances but when my life changed and the changes were painful, I found it difficult to completely surrender to the idea of God being in everything.

Psalms 138:8

'The Lord will work out his plans for my life- for your faithful love, O Lord endures forever. Don't abandon me for you made me.'

I knew that there was a boundary line in place in my heart. I had gotten close to the Lord but before he could take me further, this matter had to be dealt with. I began to read about the life of Joseph and how God's hand was on his life even though his circumstances went from bad to worse before they ever got better. When I got to where his brothers came to Egypt to buy food, Joseph revealed himself as the brother that they had sold into slavery many years before.

They were frightened that Joseph, now that he was Prime Minister of Egypt, could have them put in prison. Joseph, during his years in Egypt had kept his heart right with God, he accepted the circumstances, that didn't mean he had to like them, but in trusting God, he accepted them. His heart was compassionate towards his brothers and he wept as he embraced them and assured them that it was God who had sent him here, not them

Genesis 45:7-8

'God has sent me ahead of you to keep you and your families alive and to preserve many survivors. So, it was God who sent me here, not you. And he is the one who made me an advisor to Pharaoh-the manager of his entire palace and the governor of Egypt.'

The story of Joseph really spoke to my heart and I realised that God was taking care of me regardless of how my circumstances had changed. In accepting that God is in everything, I'm not saying that he sent all the emotional pain into my life that came about because of my wrong choices or the failure of my marriage. My God is a good God and there have been times in my life when I have made choices that led me down paths of pain yet God in his grace never left me and brought me out the other side. I have a free will and looking back over the years I know that whatever my reasons for making choices that were not God's best for me, I went into situations I shouldn't have been in and that resulted in mental and emotional pain. I want to emphasise every experience has been a huge learning curve with God and my relationship has grown with him. When I say that I am thankful for his grace, it's because he never left me and in times of great emotional and mental distress, his love and grace led me back into a deeper experience with him. I know what it is like to make mistakes, I've made more than enough but I also know what it is like to experience the grace and forgiveness of God. The times that I cried when I felt my heart was breaking, Jesus was right there beside me and he felt my pain and saw my tears. He loved me back into the perfect place of forgiveness and peace. When I say my God is a good God, believe me, He is.

In reading the life of Joseph and the difficult circumstances he found himself in, there is a sentence repeated several times in chapter 39, 'and the Lord was with Joseph.'

I realised that the Lord has always been with me and always will be. He was on my side and therein lies my security.

There could no longer be any room in my life for doubts, no if's or buts. I had to trust the Lord for all of me and every circumstance in my life. I stepped across the line and surrendered another piece of my heart. God is faithful and he never changes and that makes me feel very secure. I could trust him for everything in my life because he would always make a way for me.

Regardless of my circumstances changing, whether those changes were good or bad I knew that my God never changes, he is faithful, consistent and I could trust him with every detail that concerned me. Going forward as a single parent, life became a routine of home, work and church but my favourite times when I was at home and the children were in bed and I would be reading my bible or a book in my bed. I liked that secure feeling that we were being looked after.

I was a single parent for several years and the loneliest times were those special occasions when I would see families together and I felt like I was on the outside of something but looking in. At Christmas time when I would be shopping and I'd see a couple shopping together or I'd go into a café and see a couple sharing lunch and talking, I realised it was the little things of life that made being a single parent so difficult. I was a Christian, a working mum and a woman who sometimes felt lonely. I missed having someone to talk to, have dinner with and be close to. I missed being loved and I felt I had so much love to give.

Eventually I got involved in a relationship thinking it might lead to something more permanent, but I was wrong. I got involved because I was lonely and this person was charming and tender and although I had doubts, I still went along with it. I loved the attention, the romance and intimacy. He was Christian but I compromised my relationship with God in the hope a relationship would work out with him. I discovered how easy it is to slip into a relationship for all the wrong reasons. I say this with honesty, because I know of Christian women who have been on their own for a long time and feeling lonely is difficult to get used to. I used to feel that life was passing me by, and I would be lonely for the rest of my life. I made mistakes and when the relationship ended, I was hurt and lonelier than ever. Feeling like I was back to square one I did what I knew to do, I ran to my Father and his love and grace reached out to me and poured over me. For a time, it had felt good being a couple, but then my relationship with the Lord wasn't my priority.

When the relationship ended, I realised I shouldn't have been in it in the first place! I repented, and the Lord's forgiveness restored my peace and I was back where I belonged. I've struggled being a woman alone but then I realised that this time in my life was precious between God and me. It was a time of getting to know him more and getting to know myself.

I became more accepting of my circumstances and emotionally more content. My experience had been another learning curve in my life and my relationship with the Lord and his grace overwhelmed me because he knew I would go running back to him and he waited patiently for me because his love for me would heal the hurt and draw me close to him again.

Zephaniah 3:17

'For the Lord you God is living among you. He is a mighty Saviour. He will take delight in you with gladness, with his love he will calm all your fears. He will rejoice over you with joyful songs.'

I loved to worship and sing, and God likes nothing more than his child worshipping him, in prayer, in songs and in dance. In worship I am still inside, as my heart connects with his Holy Spirit. Supernatural peace is amazing, and it strengthened me. Sometimes in life I would get impatient because I thought God wasn't moving quick enough for me, but God is not in a hurry.

Ecclesiastes 3:11 says, 'Yet God has made everything beautiful for its own time...'

Learning to be still and trust God for my life was exciting at times but like anyone else, I had my days when I just didn't want to go on with the way life was. I had my coping strategies, I would focus on the children, the home and being organised for my work the next day. I'd have a nice bubble bath and an early night with a book, this always worked.

It was then I was thankful I was on my own. I did like my own company, but this had been another learning curve because it wasn't always like that. Even on my down days

I found something that would help to lift me up again. I had times when I was physically tired and had a busy day in work and all I wanted to do was have an early night. Now when I'm tired, I sometimes forget things and it is funny the daft things I do.

One night I was heading up to bed and I'd made a cup of tea. Having checked the doors were locked and everything was switched off, I turned off the lights and went up to bed. I thought I'd put my cup of tea on the bedside table, but it wasn't there. I went back down to the kitchen and turned on the light expecting the cup to be on the worktop but no, it wasn't there. I knew I had made it because the kettle was still warm, and I'd left the milk on the worktop. I opened the fridge to put the milk back and there on the shelf was my cup of tea! I'd put it in the fridge instead of the milk. Another time I came home with the shopping and as I was putting it away, I was thinking of what I'd do for dinner that night. Later I needed my purse, but it wasn't in my bag or anywhere else I looked. I was beginning to panic when I saw I hadn't put the oven chips in the freezer. As I went to put them in. there in the freezer was my purse. I must have been trying to freeze the pound! I'm joking about these incidents but as a single parent there was always so much on my mind and I got tired. I'm glad God blessed me with a sense of humour, and I could laugh at the silly things I did.

Proverbs 31-25

'She is clothed with strength and dignity, and she laughs without fear of the future.'

Chapter 5

In 1988 I met the man I would marry, which I did in 1989. I had all sorts of expectations for a second marriage and lots of concerns. We all have emotional baggage that can carry over from previous relationships and it's easy to assume we have learnt from past mistakes and this time it will all be different.

Falling in love was easy and my world began to change. I loved being a couple and going out for dinner or a drive in the car. Billy and I shared a similar sense of humour and we laughed a lot. We enjoyed the little things, like walking along the beach with the dog and having lunch in a nice café. I began to feel more secure and I enjoyed the sense of belonging and sharing life with another person. Billy had a son from his first marriage, Colin, and being the oldest, Julie and Paul now had a big brother and they liked that. It was good when we were all together.

Like all new relationships, in the beginning we were getting to know each other, and everything was new and exciting. When we married, we had our share of disagreements and as both of us were stubborn, we could do the silent treatment with no problem. I remember we had an argument and we were giving each other the silent treatment.

I had begun to paint a room and Billy went out to work. I got on great with what I was doing and never gave the argument a second thought. When Billy came home from work, I asked him how his day had been, and he said it was great and then we looked at each other and laughed. We were so determined that our argument would not spoil our day, yet it was obvious we were both annoyed because of it. Making up was always the best part though. Billy could be romantic, like on Valentine's day, I would get flowers delivered and a card that said, 'From someone who loves you.'

I'd phone him at work to thank him and he would pretend he didn't send the flowers and they must be from some secret admirer!

Like all relationships, our marriage had problems and we would clash over issues that we couldn't agree on. I had doubts that the marriage would last but we got over stuff and kept going. I loved when Billy was in church with me as church can be lonely when you are on your own. However, Billy struggled with church and it didn't matter what church it was, he would go for a few months and then back off from it. This resulted in arguments because I wanted him with me, but I learnt that I couldn't make him do something he didn't want to do. Billy always said that his best times with God was when he was away fishing on his own, he enjoyed fishing off the rocks and the quietness, and he always came back refreshed and sometimes shared his thoughts with me. I went with him and he taught me to fish and once I caught more than him and we had a laugh over it, I didn't like to put the bait on though, Billy got the job of putting on the ragworms.

I went to church and Billy stayed at home and while I accepted it, I missed him. I felt there was always a wedge between us because we were separate in our views. Time and experience have taught me lessons I wish I had learnt sooner. I made mistakes in my marriage and I didn't always put my husband first, Billy also made mistakes, but life is a learning curve and I'm glad we stayed together.

We used to talk about where we thought we had gone wrong in previous relationships but that led us to have a level of expectation for our marriage that we couldn't live up to. I tried to be what he wanted me to be and he tried to be the husband I wanted him to be and really, it was so silly then. It took years for us to learn to accept each other and it took the pressure off both of us. It was hard work staying married and it would have been easy to end it, but I really didn't want another divorce, besides, no matter what happened in our lives, we never stopped loving each other.

Learning to love unconditionally was not easy for me and I walked the extra mile more times than enough, in fact, I walked enough extra miles to travel a whole motorway! Well-meaning friends would suggest maybe counselling would help, but Billy and I didn't need a counsellor, we needed a referee!

Billy would tease me and say our marriage would be perfect if only I would do what I was told! As if!! He loved my independent nature and he saw me as being a strong woman, yet I thought that I should be different, and I tried to be a better wife. In trying to be the woman I thought he wanted me to be, I didn't argue with him and I was doing everything right and told myself this is the way a wife should be. I had read several books on marriage and I thought I've got this covered! One night we had a huge row over something silly and he said he didn't like the way I had changed. He had fallen in love with a strong independent woman who knew her own mind and I wasn't that person anymore. He was right, I was trying to be something that I wasn't, that soon changed! Those marriage books went straight in the bin!

Billy had another love in his life and that was his motorbike, she was called Betsy, a BMW and it was a class bike. I'd never been on a motorbike until I married Billy and at first, I was scared but then I loved it. The freedom of the open road on a lovely day took us to lots of places and Billy loved it. He kept the bike in the workshop at the back of our house and he would be out there cleaning it and checking everything on it.

I told him that he loved Betsy more than me and he said that Betsy did what she was told! Then he would laugh at the expression on my face.

Billy's other love was his boat, it was a small boat and he named it after me, Chrissie Q. We had that boat for years and we would go to Lough Erne and moored the boat there. It was lovely going out on the lough on a warm day and the fresh air cleared my head. One of our favourite places was Whitepark Bay, we loved the beach and the clear water. There was a stream that ran down through the caves and the water was so fresh and clean, it was beautiful. As the years went on our relationship got better, I was free in my relationship with God and Billy was free to be himself without me judging him. Marriage is difficult a lot of the time. Billy and I were so different in our personalities and yet he was my soulmate and I knew we would always be together.

Our relationship went through a lot of tough times and we were close to divorce more than once but I'm glad that didn't happen. It took years for us to learn to accept each other's differences but eventually we did, and life became much easier.

I loved being married but I admit, it wasn't like I thought it was going to be, it was difficult and just when I thought we had it sorted, something would flare up and the hard work would begin again. As a woman, I loved sitting in church with my husband beside me. We were together and we belonged with each other. We were on the same wavelength and it was good for our relationship. My most difficult times were when Billy decided he didn't want to go to church anymore, he had his reasons and I wasn't always understanding of why he made the decisions he made. I saw just one picture and when the picture changed, I was confused. I had my loneliest times when I went to church and my husband stayed home. Church can be a lonely place for a woman on her own. The husband that used to sit beside me wasn't there anymore and I felt like part of me was missing. There was tension at home because I resented his decision and really, I should have just left him with God and got on with my own relationship with the Lord.

I realise that I placed too much emphasis on church when my marriage should have been more of a priority. Eventually I came to a place of peace with God and my husband. I accepted that Billy enjoyed his time with the Lord when he was away fishing on his own. When I stopped resenting him, he began to share his thoughts more with me and we slowly learnt to meet in the middle. This was probably the greatest learning curve for me in my marriage and it took a long time to get there, but it was worth it.

Our family was getting on with their lives in their relationships and their jobs. Eventually we had our first grandchild and it was an amazing time. When my daughter had Dylan, it was an amazing time for Billy and me. When Dylan was born, he had dark hair and brown eyes and he was gorgeous. The first time I held him was like falling in love again. I love being a granny. As the years went on, I would be blessed with another four grandsons, Jake, Dylan's brother. My son Paul and his partner Roisin had Shea, followed by Luke and Jude. Holding a new-born baby is amazing and I am so thankful I got to experience it. I love our boys to the moon and back.

Billy enjoyed being a grandad and he looked forward to the time when he could teach the boys to fish and do the things he enjoyed doing. He had plans for when the boys were older, although plans can change, even when you don't want them to.

Chapter 6

I'd left school at fifteen without any qualifications. At that time, you could leave school on a Friday and start work on a Monday. I didn't really like school although I would have liked a career. To gain qualifications, I would have needed to stay on at school and I remember thinking that I could do that, I really believed that although I'd struggled with school, I felt that another year would have made a difference. Towards the end of my last year, my mum came along to see the careers teacher with me. I was asked what I would like to do, and I said I wanted to be a nurse. I was asked to consider something else! Mum didn't want me to stay at school as she didn't see the point of education. After all, I'd probably get married, have children and be at home anyway. I didn't feel I was good enough for a career, yet there was a little glimmer of hope in me. Unfortunately, I was the only one with the glimmer of hope. My choices were narrowed down to working in a shop, office or factory.

In my years at school, the rules were hard and caning a pupil was nothing unusual. I had my share of that! However, the most damaging were the words that were spoken by teachers who ought to have known better.

Now not all teachers are the same. I had a few favourite teachers who were encouraging and treated their pupils like human beings. I also had a few teachers that really shouldn't have been in the job. There was one teacher that I was always out to impress, I don't know why I wanted her to like me, I just did. It didn't matter what I did, she didn't like me! She was never quick to use the cane, but her words used to devastate me. She used to tell me that she knew my sort, referring to my working-class background. She said I would never be anything, would never amount to very much. I remember one day in class; she was in a good mood and I was enjoying the lesson. I got stuck on something and went up to her and asked for her help. Totally unexpected, she slapped me hard across the face. I heard some of the girl's gasp in surprise. I was shocked and couldn't speak. I was told to get out of her sight and got put in the storeroom and the door closed. Now, I remember how that felt and from that day, I stopped trying to impress her. As far as she was concerned, I was nothing and never would be. Sadly, I was already believing it. When I got home and told my mum, she told me not to worry, sure I was leaving in a few weeks.

I'm using this example because there are other people who would have experienced what I did at school. That's the way it was back then. No one knew the damage that negative words could have on a person. When I left school, I felt relieved in one sense and a failure too. Somewhere inside me I still had that glimmer of hope for something better. In later years God taught me about forgiveness and I forgave that teacher. Perhaps she had more problems than me!

I began work in Woolworths, in Belfast and I liked it. It was good to be earning money, although in those days you got your wages in a little brown envelope and I knew to take it home to my mum. I remember my dad's envelope sitting on the fireplace and mine went there too and mum gave me back a certain amount that was to last me for a week. It never did though, and she would give me money the day before payday the next week.

I was there less than a year when I got the opportunity to work in an office that was closer to home. I preferred office work as I had the weekend off and that was something to look forward to. I continued working in clerical work until I had my daughter and then two years later, I had Paul.

When my marriage broke up and I went back to work, I did clerical work and as one temporary job came to an end, I worked in a shop, another office and a cleaning job in a hospital. During my years as a single parent I did all sorts of jobs and I was registered with several job agencies as I did temporary work rather than be unemployed. By the time I'd married again, and the children were teenagers, I decided it was time I had an education. There were certain jobs that I wanted to do but I wasn't qualified even though reading the job description I knew I could do the job. At age thirty-nine I began by doing GCSE English language and literature. I loved it. It awakened something in me that had been asleep for too long. I followed that up with business administration and computers. This gave me a foundation in basic qualifications. As my interest lay in social welfare, I then did a counselling diploma before enrolling with open university.

With each course I did, my confidence grew and I was able to apply for jobs with bigger salaries. I enrolled on a degree course in health and social welfare and at first, I was apprehensive as I'd not studied at university level before. However, I soon got into the way of studying and I enjoyed it so much. My brain felt like a sponge, soaking it all up and I loved the tutorials on a Saturday morning. Adult education was nothing like being at school and my desire to learn and develop skills continued to grow. I was apprehensive about my first exam with O.U. but I passed, and I was excited about my second year. Everything I ever wanted was happening for me and I knew with the right qualifications I could get a better job and a better salary, so I had a goal. I did my second year and passed my next exam and prepared for my third year. I'd worked in several community-based jobs while I was studying, and I loved helping people. I found an identity through my work and my confidence had grown as I gained new skills.

My goal was to finish my degree and get into a permanent job that would see me through until retirement. It felt great to have a goal and to make plans. At times I remembered my desire to be a writer and it was still there but I was so busy with this new me that writing had to be put on hold, but I knew I'd get back to it at some point, I just didn't know when.

I did keep a journal and recorded my thoughts to the Lord in it but my priorities in life were education and career, I also had a family and a husband. My life was so busy, and I thrived on it.

In July 1997 I was working in a community group and I'd just finished work at 5pm. I was glad to be finishing work as my daughter was graduating from Queens University the next day. She had been studying law and I was looking forward to her big day. I had booked time off work and I was excited for my daughter.

I left the building I was working in and I noticed it had been raining earlier on, I hoped it wouldn't rain the next day. I got to the top of the steps and reached out to take the handrail when I went over on my ankle. I tried to keep hold of the rail, but it was slippery with the rain. I lost my balance and began to fall forward down the flight of concrete steps. I must have turned over because I landed on my back and hit my head of the ground. I lay there for a few seconds and at first, I couldn't feel anything. Another member of staff who was with me, helped me up as the pain began to kick in. I knew I'd hurt my back, but I hoped it was just bruised. I refused to go to the hospital. I got home and took painkillers, had a bath and went to bed. The next morning the pain was bad, but I decided to take painkillers with me and stay focussed on the main event.

We had a lovely day and I was so proud of Julie as she was awarded her degree and afterwards, we went for a meal. When I got home, I was exhausted and went to bed. The pain had got worse but at least I could rest now. Early the next morning the pain in my lower spine woke me up and I knew that I had to get to the hospital.

I had x-rays and blood tests and thankfully my spine wasn't fractured but I'd damaged tissue and I had to rest and take painkillers until it healed. I remember the shock of falling down the steps had frightened me and for a few days after it, I felt quiet inside. The doctor had said that trauma would make me feel that way but in time I should be alright. Eventually I went back to work but the pain in my spine never went away and I was tired all the time.

The things I enjoyed doing became an effort and I knew that something was wrong with me. It was like I'd never fully recovered from the fall. I changed jobs and I loved my new post in the community, however I found that walking a short distance made the pain in my spine worse and now it was going down my leg. I went to the doctor and I was referred to Musgrave Park Hospital in Belfast. I was to have an MRI scan, but it took a long time for the appointment, meanwhile life rolled on. I continued to work but I experienced pain every day and the fatigue left me with no strength. I would come home from work and sleep. The doctor prescribed painkillers, which helped but I was so tired I just wanted to be in bed. There was nothing else that could be done until I'd had a scan and I was still on the waiting list. I stayed in work because I loved my job and everyday was different. I enjoyed community work because I was in contact with people who needed help and encouragement and I felt it was the right job for me.

In December, my dad had a fall at home and had to go into hospital. He had fractured his lower spine and was in a lot of pain. Dad was eighty-one and was rarely sick. He didn't retire from work until he was seventy-five and since he was at home, his health slowly began to deteriorate. I went with him to the hospital for x-rays, we went by ambulance and on arrival my dad hadn't been able to walk. The staff got me a wheelchair and I walked down the corridor to the x-ray department. It felt strange wheeling dad in a wheelchair. My dad had worked most of his life and he also loved to walk. To see him in pain and not able to walk was upsetting. I knew he was in pain, but Dad never liked to complain. I was able to take him home but a few days later he had to go back. It was then we were told he had fractured his spine. We hoped with bed rest and medication he would be home soon but then we were told he would be in for Christmas. I was upset over this and so was the rest of the family. Christmas that year was different. We went to visit him in the afternoon, and he was trying to put on a brave face. We took presents and my sister Sharon brought up a turkey dinner in case he didn't like the hospital food.

We took photographs and tried to make the best of the situation. I felt depressed when I came home. I had this feeling that more changes were going to happen, and I was worried they would concern my Dad.

I loved my job; it was based in the community and I was a project worker who visited people in their homes. I enjoyed the work, and that I got to meet different people. Each day was different, and I liked that. The one thing that hindered me was the pain I was still experiencing in my lower back. When I got home from work, I was so tired I just wanted to sleep. I knew there was something wrong with me, but my GP had done all he could and until I got a hospital appointment, I had to endure the pain. With my Dad in hospital, I went to work and went to the hospital at night and that's about all I could manage. The family had a rota for the hospital, so I didn't go every night.

Dad seemed to be making progress and we were hoping he could come home soon, then one day night the family got a call to go to the hospital. Dad had an infection and he was struggling to breathe. I sat beside him as the doctor tried to take blood from his vein, but he was so ill, his veins had collapsed. Finally, they got it from his wrist, but he was in pain and I put my arms around him and held him as he continued to struggle with his breathing. The rest of the family came back in and I went out for a few minutes. I didn't like what was happening and I was scared we were going to lose him that night. After a few hours he settled and his breathing was normal, he was exhausted, and I felt he had fought for his life that night. I got home after three and fell into bed.

The next morning, I phoned the hospital and Dad had improved a little. He was on an intravenous drip which was an antibiotic and he had slept. The crisis had passed, but I was on edge.

When the infection had passed, Dad could only talk in a whisper. His vocal cords were damaged, and he was still in decline. When I would ask him if he were okay, he would smile and nod his head.

He was quiet and would sometimes close his eyes and rest for a few minutes. I was okay when I was with him but when I got home, I still had this feeling of dread. I was glad that dad and I had a better relationship and the days of arguments ended with my teenage years.

The one thing that bothered me was that I'd never told my Dad I loved him, and I can't ever remember him saying it to me. Dad grew up in a time when people didn't talk to each other about how they felt and when I was growing up, I knew I was loved by my parents, but we didn't talk about it. I prayed about this because it really was bothering me. When I talked to the Lord about it, I had the assurance in my heart that there would be an opportunity for me to tell Dad that I loved him.

Later in the week I was up at the hospital with Mum, and Dad was sitting in the chair at the side of his bed. He was quiet and tired. Usually when we were leaving, he would ask me to get the nurse to help him into bed but that night he asked me to help him. As I got him into bed, Mum walked to the entrance of the ward. I knew this was my opportunity. I got him into bed, fixed his pillows and covered him with his duvet. As I went to kiss him on the cheek, he looked at me and smiled. Dad had the loveliest blue eyes. I looked at him and said, 'Dad I love you.' He smiled and said, 'I love you too.' I kissed his cheek and left. I turned and waved back to him and he was watching me. He waved and then settled back on his pillows and closed his eyes. I was at peace that night when I got home, and I was thankful that God had answered prayer for me.

I was tired and after a cup of tea I went to bed. I slept and it was a deep sleep where my body and mind were rested. I awoke around five and Dad was my first thought. I began to pray and to worship God. In worship, I was aware of his presence and I was strengthened as I prayed. In relationship with the Lord, I am heart to heart with him, worship connects me deeper and the Holy Spirit takes me to that place where only the presence of the Lord matters. Nothing or no one else can compare with the depth of his love for me.

Isaiah 32:17 'And this righteousness will bring peace. Yes, it will bring quietness and confidence forever.'

As I prayed for my Dad. I saw in my spirit, a picture of Dad, in a lovely suit, my Dad liked nice clothes. He was running up a road. The road was dark and there were trees on either side. Dad was focused on getting up this road and this was his goal. I was surprised he was running because Dad couldn't walk very well since he fractured his spine, but he clearly was running. I could see he was running towards a light and the closer he got to it the brighter it became. Eventually he ran into it and he was gone. I realised then that we were losing Dad and that heaven was his home. I thanked God for allowing me to see this as it helped to prepare me, but for now Dad was still with us and I was at peace. I continued to visit the hospital with the family, but Dad was deteriorating.

On Wednesday twenty sixth of February, Dad woke up early in the morning. A nurse came to check on him and he said he was hungry. The nurse brought him a bowl of cereal, which he enjoyed and then he went back to sleep. At eight thirty, when the breakfasts were being served, the nurse spoke to him and he smiled, then his colour changed, and she knew something was wrong. Dad was going into cardiac arrest. The doctors responded quickly and tried to save him, but he was gone.

I got a phone call at work to go to the hospital and when I arrived the doctor was waiting. She told me Dad had died and how it had happened. I went in and sat with him while I waited for the family to arrive. He looked so peaceful and I was thankful his suffering was over. Sitting there quietly,

I had to smile. My dad loved his food and he had eaten his cereal early that morning. He died just as the breakfast was being served, but he hadn't missed out on his! He was eighty-one and he had gone home to heaven, to a new life of health and freedom.

The family got together with Mum to make the funeral arrangements. I was looking through my Dad's bible and he had marked out a verse in Isaiah.

Isaiah 60:1 'Arise, shine, for your light has come, and the glory of the Lord rises upon you.'

I remembered the picture I saw of Dad running up a road and then running into the light and I knew that he had gone to be with the Lord, and he was now basking in the glory of God. The funeral was peaceful and dignified and people came back to my Mum's house afterwards. It was February and it was cold so several of the family had made big pots of homemade vegetable soup and there were lots of bread rolls. There was so much food in my Mum's house. It's like a tradition that when someone dies everyone who calls at the house brings food!

I knew that Dad was gone yet, I was aware of how death changed things. I would no longer see Dad sitting on the sofa with his newspaper. He would never see his favourite football team play again. The family had lost a Dad, but the grandchildren had lost their grandad. Nothing would ever be the same, but it would be different. A link in the family chain had been broken and while I know that death is a part of life, when it happens to a parent then it changes the dynamics in the family. Dad had gone and now Mum was on her own and she also had health problems.

Dad had now reached the destination of the Christian life and he was in heaven. I'm glad I have the security of knowing I will see him again and while death is the end of this life, it's the beginning of a new one that one day we all would experience. Losing Dad also brought home to me that life is short, and I realised that I sometimes took life for granted. I'd put things off to another time, as if I had all the time in the world. It took a long time for me to accept dad was gone and I was aware of the gap in the family now. Mum's life had changed too and she had to get used to being the only one in the house.

There is that time of adjustment when someone close dies and for me, the reality of life never being the same. Dad was gone from this life, although he now had a new one. He loved to be in the garden, and I wonder if he has his own garden in heaven where the flowers never die, and he can enjoy walking through the grass surrounded by angels.

I miss Dad at times, and I know when we are united again in heaven when we will love and laugh as we enjoy the presence of Jesus for all eternity.

Matthew 5:1-10

One day as he saw the crowds gathering, Jesus went up on the mountainside and sat down. His disciples gathered around him, and he began to teach them.

'God blesses those who are poor and realise their need of him, for the kingdom of heaven is theirs.

God blesses those who mourn, for they shall be comforted.

God blesses those who are humble, for they shall inherit the whole earth.

God blesses those who hunger and thirst for justice, for they will be satisfied.

God blesses those who are merciful for they will be shown mercy.

God blesses those whose hearts are pure, for they will see God.

God blesses those who work for peace, for they will be called the children of God.

God blesses those who are persecuted for doing right, for the Kingdom of heaven is theirs.'

Chapter 7

After my Dad died, I had some time of work to rest. I was still in pain with my back and I felt exhausted. I can cope with a situation at the time but when it is over, I seem to go down physically with exhaustion and pain. I slept a lot and just wanted to be quiet. I visited my Mum and I found it strange being in the house and dad not there. Usually he sat on the sofa with his newspaper.

As a family we tried to help Mum move on with her life. There is so much to do after someone dies. The paperwork and form filling we could help with. Pensions had to be sorted and other benefits. It can be exhausting for the person left behind. Mum had been having health problems for years so she needed as much help as the family could give her. As she was the only one in the house now, we talked to her about moving to somewhere smaller, but it would have been too much of an upheaval for her. She had visitors most days in the week and we arranged different days for different people.

The family had to go back to their jobs and they too were coping with losing Dad. I was aware that the dynamics had changed and that takes some getting used to for everyone. Grief affects people differently and they need to have the space to grieve in their own way. I returned to work and it helped to get back into the work routine every day. I was experiencing a lot of pain and when I got home from work, I would fall asleep on the sofa. I couldn't figure out how the fall I'd had that injured my spine, now caused the pain to go down my legs and the fatigue had me exhausted. I went back to the doctor and had more blood tests done and was sent to physio. I was then sent to the pain clinic at the hospital for spinal injections which helped for a short time but eventually the pain would return worse than ever. I was still on the waiting list for an MRI scan and until then there wasn't anything else, I could do.

The one joy in my life was my studies. I did my second-year exams with Open University and passed, which was so good. In my job I got the practical experience I needed to help with my social welfare course and then my studies gave me the theory. I was deciding on the following years subjects when life took a different turn.

My employer knew I'd been experiencing health problems and they had been good at giving me time for appointments. My contract for this job was a yearly contract which was about to be renewed. I had a meeting with H.R. which is normal procedure but to my surprise my contract wasn't being renewed, I was being let go. They were letting me go on medical grounds which meant I would get benefits straight away, but it was a shock losing my job. Suddenly my career plans were gone as my job and my course went together. Being dismissed on health grounds also meant I couldn't get another job unless my health improved. My employer understood the health issues and they were sympathetic, but the truth was, I couldn't do my job and I had been struggling for a while. I left work before lunch time that day and said goodbye to the staff.

I arrived home and just sat down on the sofa and couldn't think straight. Knowing my job had gone would affect my career, my finances and my mental health. Having a job and doing my degree gave me a focus but now it felt like the rug had been pulled out from under me.

I had that feeling of loss, like a part of me had just been taken away. I was still grieving the loss of my dad and now I'd lost something that was a big part of my life. I felt totally empty. For the first time in my life I wondered what the future would hold because from where I was sitting there was nothing to focus on. I went to see the doctor a few days later and he was surprised I'd still been working. He went over the test results and the physio report and then he told me that although I had injured my spine in the fall the spread of pain over my body was called fibromyalgia. An appointment was made to see a Consultant at Musgrave Park Hospital.

I had never heard of fibromyalgia, but I thought that now he knows what's wrong with me, I can get a prescription and make it all better. The doctor looked serious as he went on to explain there was no medical cure for this. Suddenly I realised what he was telling me, and I felt another shock hit me. I would have to get used to pain relief and exercise and I would also be given an antidepressant to help with sleep and nerve pain. I sat there thinking, there is no cure for this. It wouldn't kill me, but it would affect my mobility, my sleep, my mental health and I would have to learn to live with it.

I left the surgery with a prescription that read like a shopping list! I walked down the road and as I was about to cross, a bus was coming and just for a second I wanted to walk out in front of it, then I thought I couldn't do that to the driver! I think I was in shock for several days because I felt numb inside. I'd wake up in the morning and I wasn't motivated to do anything. The medication was making me tired, but it did ease the pain, so I had to keep taking it. I still found it hard to believe that I could no longer work, and the doctor had been surprised I was still working at all.

I did remember months before this, the same doctor had told me to give up work but of course I didn't listen. Now I had no other option. I realised I would have to decide regarding my course as I hadn't chosen any subjects for the following year. I knew without my job I couldn't really do the course and I'd been told I couldn't work again so what was the point?

I phoned student support and explained my situation and decided to withdraw from the degree course. I was so upset over this. I loved what I'd been doing, and this was another thing taken away from me. I found myself becoming quiet inside which I put down to the medication I was on, but I felt myself hitting rock bottom. There had been too much loss in a short space of time, and I didn't know how to cope with it. I went back to the doctor as I thought I was having a breakdown. He assured me I wasn't, but I was now grieving for what I had lost, and I needed to give myself time to adjust to the changes. I was tired and he told me my body and mind needed to rest and that is what I had to do. I went home and slept on the sofa and it was dark when I woke up.

I told my family what was wrong with me and they had never heard of fibromyalgia either, but I tried to make light of it because there was nothing no one could do to make it better. The one person I seemed to be avoiding was God!

I woke early one morning, and I began to pray, yet all I could say was,

'Where are you God?'

Inside I was crying out for answers and yet, there was silence. For five years I had completed so many courses to further my education, I had dreams of a career and a good salary and I was headed in the right direction but now, it was wiped away.

'Where are you God?'

I found it hard to accept that all the plans that I'd made for my career and my future salary had been taken away. The chapter on my work life had now been closed and I didn't want this. My vision was to establish a career and work until retirement and enjoy the financial benefits that came with that. Now there would be no salary. My dreams for that part of my life were over. Now I would have to learn to manage on government benefits and oh my, that would be a whole new battle to get what I was entitled to. My world had been turned upside down and I stayed in a state of unbelief for a while because I didn't know how to face whatever was in front of me.

'Where are you God?'

I felt like my life was in two halves. One half was accepting of the illness and I had to get on with life. I hoped I was giving the impression that I was managing this. I went to church and visited my Mum, who was still getting used to Dad not being there. I played down what I was really feeling in front of my family. Then there was the other half of me that felt hopeless. My sense of purpose was gone, and I was empty inside.

'Where are you God?'

The depression hit me like a train and I just didn't want to get out of bed. Pain usually woke me up and I was struggling with the fatigue. I was on various drugs as I tried to balance pain management and there was this awful sense of hopelessness because I'd been told that this is the way my life would be. There was no medical cure and I could forget about going back to work again. I felt the rug was truly pulled out from under me and there was nothing I could do to change things.

'Where are you God?'

Every day I was searching for some solution and there wasn't one. I began to pray because I couldn't accept what was happening to me and I felt God was far away.

Isaiah 42:13 'For I hold you by your right hand, I, the Lord your God, And I say to you, 'Don't be afraid, I am here to help you.'

I realised that God hadn't left me, he hadn't moved, he was closer than ever. I was grieving and not just for my Dad, but the loss of a career and it was more than that. I'd worked hard to get as far as I did and now it seemed it was all for nothing.

Surely there had to be a purpose to my life. I was sad as I withdrew from my course and put my books away. It was like I was packing away the dreams I had and with a sigh, I knew that part of my life was over. I had made my peace with God as I realised, I needed him more than ever.

I decided to begin writing and planned out a few new projects. If I couldn't work outside the home, then maybe I could do something in the home. I sent off sample chapters of a story to different agents and publishers and I got one rejection letter after another. I became so frustrated with life. I couldn't be content to do nothing. Just when I thought I could begin to climb another ladder of success; I'd slide right now to the bottom. I still liked to write though, so I kept up with writing in my journal, even though it seemed quite depressing at times. I told myself that things would improve and if I kept writing I was sure to have something accepted eventually.

I finally got to have the MRI scan and after another long wait I saw a consultant. There was tissue damage to my lower spine, and I might need surgery in the future. He confirmed the fibromyalgia diagnosis as I had thirteen out of eighteen trigger points over my body. Years later I now have all eighteen.

Fibromyalgia affects my whole body and the trigger points are pain points that if pressed would be very painful for me. Sometimes my muscles go into spasm. These are very painful, especially when it wakes me out of a sleep! Fibromyalgia also affects sleep as it is difficult to get into a deep sleep and the result is fatigue the next day. It also affects my mental health and there is this ongoing battle with depression. 'Fibro fog' is another symptom and I can be forgetful as my brain feels fogged up and I can't think clearly. Now at times the 'fibro fog' results in me doing silly things, like putting things in the wrong place and not being able to remember it. One time I thought I put the washing in the machine but when I went to start the wash there was nothing there! I retraced my steps thinking I'd left it in the bedroom, then the bathroom, but no, I couldn't find the washing. Beside the machine is a swing top bin and you can guess where my washing was. I'd put it in the bin. I did laugh at this, yet, it wasn't funny, not really. It was just another symptom of this horrible illness.

As a Christian I had people who prayed for me and supported me, but I came up against a new problem. Having been prayed for, people would ask me why I was still in pain. I was told to 'walk it out.' Sorry, I had days when I couldn't walk round the house! I know people meant well because they wanted to see me healed and getting past this.

But I felt a failure as a Christian. I began to question my faith. Maybe I didn't have enough faith or maybe there was something wrong with me spiritually that was stopping my healing. I wasted so much time taking myself apart, looking for some secret sin, wasted precious energy fighting against the pain only to make the pain much worse. I wanted God to put me in his microwave and after two minutes I'd come out all healed and made whole, ready to take on the world. I would write about a miraculous healing and then put the past behind me and go and get a job. My doctors would be astonished at my recovery and I'd return all my drugs to the pharmacy as I wouldn't need them anymore. It didn't happen. I didn't know if I was disappointed in myself or God, I know, imagine being disappointed with God!

At times like this I had to learn that my enemy was still out to rob, steal and destroy and having doubts about my relationship with God was dangerous ground for me to be on. I finally got to the place of accepting that God was with me in my circumstances and I had to trust him for each day. He still had a purpose in my life, even if I didn't always see it. I got back to reading books and my bible and writing in my journal and it helped me in so many ways as it gave me something positive to focus on. Taking each new day as it arrived became a new learning curve but one, I travelled with God. I began to focus on scriptures that helped me through, and I kept believing that God created me, and his will was for me to be healed physically and made whole in every way.

Psalm 27:7,8,13-14

Hear me as I pray, O Lord. Be merciful and answer me! My heart has heard you say, 'Come and talk with me.'

And my heart responds, 'Lord I am coming.'

Yet I am confident I will see the Lord's goodness while I am here in the land of the living. Wait, patiently for the Lord. Be brave and courageous. Yes, wait patiently for the Lord.

Psalm 103:1-5

Let all that I am praise the Lord; with my whole heart, I will praise his holy name. Let all that I am praise the Lord; may I never forget the good things he does for me. He forgives all my sins and heals all my diseases.

He redeems me from death and crowns me with love and tender mercies. He fills my life with good things. My youth is renewed like the eagle's!

Jeremiah 17:14

O Lord, if you heal me, I will be truly healed; if you save me, I will be truly saved. My praises are for you alone.!

Isaiah 38:16

Lord, your discipline is good, for it leads to life and health. You restore my health and allow me to live.

Malachi 4:6

But for you who fear my name, the Sun of Righteousness will rise with healing in his wings. And you will go free, leaping with joy like calves let out to pasture.

Matthew 4:23

Jesus travelled throughout the region of Galilee, teaching in the synagogues and announcing the Good News about the kingdom. And he healed every kind of disease and illness.

1 Peter 2:21-25

For God called you to do good, even if it means suffering, just as Christ suffered for you. He is your example, and you must follow in his steps. He never sinned, nor deceived anyone. He did not retaliate when he was insulted, nor threaten revenge when he suffered. He left his case in the hands of God, who always judges fairly. He personally carried our sins in his body on the cross so that we can be dead to sin and live for what is right. By his wounds you are healed. Once you were like sheep who wandered away. But now you have turned to your Shepherd, the Guardian of your souls.

Chapter 8

Life moved on and settled into a pattern. I had spent so much time going to hospital appointments, I went to physiotherapy, x-rays and scans and finally it came down to pain management with the help of drugs and when necessary, injections. I might have to have surgery later but the plan for now was learning to manage pain in my everyday life and rest when the fatigue was bad. Wow, I hadn't signed up for this and part of me was still angry at what had happened. Being reduced to sickness benefit when I used to have a salary took a lot of getting used to. I was thankful Billy was working and we managed, but I missed working and having more money coming in. Billy was more accepting of my being at home than I was. He liked coming home from work to a warm house, coffee on and bread fresh from the bread maker and I liked it too, but I'd had ambitions that weren't going to happen now. It was like something that used to be had now gone.

I missed having the routine of a working life, so I had to create a new one. Some days I'd be at home and do stuff and I had other days when I would go into town or visit Mum. She had health problems too but when she was able, we would go into town and have something to eat in the Pancake House. Mum loved their cherry pancakes with fresh cream, I did too even though they were loaded with calories. Mum loved going around the shops and looking at purses and handbags, she always had quite a collection. We always went to a book shop and came out with books; it would have been a sin not to!

Mum used to love going out on her own too but then she developed vertigo and had several falls, this affected her confidence and she was afraid to go out alone. During the winter months her health declined due to asthma and chest infections. She struggled on her own and I think she missed having Dad in the house, although she would never admit to this. I remember she kept a photo of him in a frame and it sat on the shelf of the display cabinet in the living room. One afternoon when I visited her, she wasn't in good form that day. She was being grumpy about something that Dad used to do that annoyed her and she kept looking at his photo as she complained. I laughed at her because although Dad was no longer with us, Mum still told him off. Later that day, she fell asleep in the chair and a loud bang woke her up. Dad's photo had fallen off the shelf onto the floor, the frame wasn't broken, and we never found out how it had fallen but the next time I was in her house, I noticed his picture was missing off the shelf. She told the story of it falling so she just put it on the table upstairs, dad was banished from the living room!

I loved spring and summer as the warmer weather helped with the level of pain I was in. Life was easier for me in the warmer days. I seemed to have more energy in the summer months, and it felt good to enjoy life more. Billy loved to go fishing and we would go for a drive up round the coast where he would fish off the rocks for a few hours. I would relax in the sun with a book and enjoy the heat. We had a small boat at that time, and we would go up to Carrybridge and take the boat out on Lough Erne. I loved this place; it was peaceful, and the fresh air cleared my head. This was our relaxing time.

We stayed at the Carrybridge hotel at night and had lovely meals there. We slept on the boat once, well, once was enough for me. I like a comfortable bed, a warm shower in the morning and breakfast before spending a day on the lough. Billy had a name plate made for the boat, he called it after me, Chrissie Q; the Q was for queen. The summer months went so quickly but we enjoyed our time at Lough Erne.

I eventually accepted that my life had changed regarding having a career and furthering my education. At home I began to read more and to write in my journal. I hoped to be able to publish a book one day but for now I enjoyed keeping a journal and reading a lot.

When I lost my job, my purpose in life had ended at that time. There was no longer a career, or a salary and education came to a halt. I knew as a person I was a wife, mother and daughter but I felt I'd lost me. It took awhile for me to realise that my identity is in my relationship with God and even though I tried to find satisfaction in other ways there was a loneliness inside me that only God could fill. I'm my Father's child and Jesus is the rock-solid foundation that my life is built upon. Knowing this is one thing but learning to live it every day is another. At times in my life I liked to be the one who is always available for everyone else if they need me. My identity was taken up in being a wife, mother and daughter but then I felt overwhelmed by other people's needs. My relationship with God was not always the priority yet now he was teaching me that my life is in him and everything else comes after that and in that way, I will have the energy for life.

I sometimes got distracted when my mind began to focus on circumstances that have been difficult and painful, and I wondered why God didn't answer prayer the way I'd have liked him to. Doubts would assail my mind and my heart would be burdened but then when I looked at the bigger picture I see that the Lord has always made a way for me because my God is a good God, no matter what, he is good and he knows what is best for me.

My trust and security are in him and I haven't always found it easy to trust but when I have reached that moment of surrender, my heart feels lighter. Walking in relationship with the Lord gives me the love and security of knowing he has me covered. I remember seeing a cartoon picture a long time ago and a little boy is being picked on by bullies and he stands up to them and says, 'you mess with me and my dad will mess with you.' I'm so glad that God is my Father and he knows all about me and looks out for me.

Psalm 27:1-2

'The Lord is my light and my salvation- so why should I be afraid? The Lord is my fortress, protecting me from danger, so why should I tremble?'

1 Peter 5:6-7

So humble yourselves under the mighty power of God, and at the right time he will lift you up in honour. Give all your worries and cares to God, for he cares for you.

Chapter 9

Mum's health continued to decline in subtle ways. She was prone to chest infections and she suffered with vertigo which meant she fell frequently. We spent a lot of time in the hospital when she had fallen and needed stitches. She spent more time at home and only went out if she had to. She became depressed and her moods would vary. I would never know how she was going to be until I arrived at her house. Some days she was in great form and other days I couldn't say or do anything to please her. She became more forgetful and then she would get frustrated because she couldn't remember something, or she would tell me the same story several times because she didn't remember saying it in the first place.

All the early signs of dementia can be easy to dismiss. Putting the remote control down and forgetting where she put it was enough to send mum into a panic, but I just thought she was a little forgetful. Her mood swings got worse and she was referred to a day hospital at the Royal Hospital.

I went with her and we were there for hours as they carried out different tests to see how good her memory was. They did other tests to check her out physically as well as psychologically. The report showed she had a decline in memory, but she could cope in other ways in her everyday life. As a family we continued to visit her and help her where we could. I watched her deteriorate over time. In slow subtle ways I could see she was struggling. She was more often experiencing low mood and could be depressed yet she had other days when her mood was great, and she would be happy. Everything about her mental state was so unpredictable. Other family members that visited her also recognised a decline in her mental health.

As the months went by, I sensed I was losing her because once on this path of dementia, there is no coming back from it. Mum used to go out to church faithfully every week yet now she was the opposite and didn't want to go out at all. As a family we made sure she had plenty of food in and we checked her medications every week. Her housework was done for her by my younger sister who liked to do that for Mum, Sharon would arrive armed with her vacuum cleaner! On the weekends, my brother and sister-in law visited and during the week the rest of the family made sure someone was there every day. We all wanted to help Mum in any way but over time we were exhausted. I had health problems with fibromyalgia and fatigue and I was experiencing pain in my lower spine. Yet no matter how I was feeling I had to be there for Mum. It was the same for the rest of the family, Mum's needs were the priority.

To help with Mum's physical needs we had some adaptations made to the house. Safety rails outside the back door where there were steps, a walk-in shower in the bathroom and a chair lift, as she got breathless going upstairs. The lift was in the living room and went up to the back bedroom. My young nephew Christopher loved getting into it and closing the door, pushing a button and going up through the ceiling to the back bedroom. We thought it was great fun. Mum was a little apprehensive in the beginning, but she got used to it after a while.

One day she got into it and as it began to move upwards, it suddenly stopped. Mum got into a panic and thought she would be stuck there and in her confusion she was afraid. I was there that day and all I had to do was push the button again and the lift moved. Mum decided that she wasn't going to go in it anymore, but she found a use for it. At night she liked to take a flask of water, teabags and biscuits up to her room, everything she needed she put on a tray. When she woke up in the middle of the night, she didn't have to go downstairs. The lift in the living room became the means of transporting anything she wanted to take upstairs and it wasn't just her tray either. When she managed to do the laundry, she would set the dry clothes in the lift and push the button and send them upstairs. She would struggle to walk up the stairs and had to use an inhaler to help her breathe but everything else in the house got the lift! I used to laugh at the things she did and when she was in good form it was a great visit, unfortunately those days were becoming few and far between. It was the same for the rest of the family, none of us knew how mum would be until we arrived to visit, and we were all becoming more concerned about her.

In caring for Mum, we made sure she was able to take her medication when needed. We would put her tablets in little containers, and she knew what to take at night-time when no one else was there. We covered every need and tried to make life as easy and comfortable for Mum and for a time that worked.

Mum would begin her day having a cup of tea in her bedroom and reading her bible and she would write verses into a notebook. She had been doing this for years and this was her time to talk to the Lord and even though she was ill, she had her time to read and pray every day. It was good she still had a focus and her love of books never faded either.

As time went on, Mum became more confused and frightened about things that wouldn't have usually bothered her. Her memory was deteriorating slowly, yet enough for the family to notice the difference.

The warning signs that her safety came into question was when she went out into the street late at night and thought she was going somewhere. Although she was right at her front garden she would panic and feel she was lost. At times the neighbours had to take her in and phone the family. In her confused state she didn't realise that she was at her front door. The feeling of being lost frightened her and it was upsetting for the family.

In January 2003, the family doctor decided to send out a social worker to chat to Mum and assess her situation. My sister Ruth was with her that day and Mum was in an argumentative mood. It was a difficult day. No matter how positive Ruth tried to be about Mum and how well she was looked after, Mum was determined to let the social worker know how hard her life was. She was advised not to go out on her own but with a member of the family, but Mum insisted she would go out whenever she liked, and she didn't need anyone. She was confused and found it difficult to answer questions, so she just made up her own answers. The social worker was concerned about leaving her so she offered her a place in respite care for a few weeks to see if it would help her. It would also give the family breathing space until she was seen by a doctor.

Later that day I received a phone call to say Mum was in a care home and I was shocked. I knew her condition had worsened but to realise that the social worker was concerned enough about her safety to suggest this brought home to me just how serious Mum's condition was. I cried when I put the phone down. None of us wanted this for Mum but then we thought it would be for two weeks only.

The next morning, I went to the care home to visit Mum and she wasn't doing good. Her mood was extremely low and when she saw me, she asked what I wanted and what I was doing there. I knew it was going to be a hard visit. She had been in the dining room when I arrived and then we went to her room. I tried to be positive and assure her, but she wasn't having it. She demanded I take her home and I'd have loved too but the sad truth was she wasn't safe on her own. The family even thought of staying at night with her but that wouldn't have stopped her getting out.

Her mind was so confused at times that she also didn't believe what we would tell her. I left her that day with a heavy heart and cried when I got home. I had that feeling deep inside me that this was the beginning of the end. I prayed and pleaded with God not to let this happen, but the reality is, in life bad things happen, unpleasant things happen, people we love get sick and die. The world we live in is a broken world, it's not the perfect world that God first created. At some time, our lives will be over and none of us know how or when, but it will happen. I was now watching my mum struggle with every little task and forget how to do the simplest things. I didn't want this for her, none of the family did.

When I got home that day, I was upset, and I wanted to be on my own and talk to God. Now I talk to God just like I talk to any person because that's called relationship! I was upset, annoyed and angry and incredibly sad and storming the gates of heaven wasn't going to change that! I knew deep in my heart that my Mum was on a journey that there would be no coming back from and that frightened me. The family were upset and worried and I felt a huge weight hanging over us. I was hoping that a few weeks in respite care would help Mum because she would be receiving care 24/7 as she needed it. I realised that the family, including myself had been worried about Mum for a long time and just didn't know how to help her, but then we didn't know what was wrong. That first week Mum was in care, everyone confused and upset. We wanted to do whatever to help her, but we really didn't know what we were dealing with. Mum had plenty of visitors and each one found her mood to be different, she could be in a happy, friendly mood or she could be depressed and wanting to blame us all for putting her in a home. It was horrendous for all of us and very confusing for Mum.

The care staff in the home were the best and Mum's medical needs were a priority. A doctor was brought in to assess her and did some tests with her. He tested her memory skills and then he arranged for a brain scan to be done at the Mater hospital.

When the results came back, we went to the home for a meeting with her social worker and the doctor, we were told that she had vascular dementia and areas of her brain showed there was damage. There is no cure for this horrible disease, but they could give her medication to try and slow it down. One thing they were clear about, Mum could no longer live independently, and she would have to remain in care. This was a huge shock to us as a family because none of us realised the extent of this illness. Vascular dementia is a very subtle illness and it creeps along with symptoms that we had been attributing to other things, for example, Mum losing the remote control for the television and not remembering where she put it and then a family member would find it beside her chair or under the cushion. It was a combination of little things, forgetfulness, confusion and mood changes. No one in the family history had dementia so we weren't thinking along those lines. Yet, now, faced with the test results, the facts were plain. Mum wasn't going to get better from this, in fact she would get worse as her brain continued to deteriorate. It would be impossible to try and explain the nature of this illness to mum, she wouldn't understand, and it would have frightened her. I remember walking out of that meeting and thinking, surely there must be something that could be done, denial was my first reaction. This was my Mum, who loved her books and her DVD's of Daniel O'Donnell and who loved to sing and now we were being told she had dementia. I knew that from here on in, life was going to be quite different.

As a family we made sure that Mum had plenty of visits and we took it in turns to go on different days. On the weekends, my brother and sister-in-law would come and take mum out in the car for a drive and stop somewhere for ice cream. Mum always liked that. The one thing all the family quickly realised was that none of us could predict what frame of mind she would be in whenever we arrived! I had days when Mum would be in great form and it would be a good visit and she would lead me to the door when I was going home and give me a hug. I also had other days when her mood was depressive and no matter how hard I tried; I couldn't help her. It was like she couldn't help herself and I was sad as I watched this horrible illness begin to take hold.

She was on lots of medication and I was never sure if any of it was helping. This illness was progressive, and nothing was going to stop it. Confusion and memory loss were one of the biggest problems I noticed with Mum. At times she remembered she had her house and then she demanded to know why I couldn't take her home and when I couldn't take her, she would do the same with the next family member that visited. She needed someone or something to blame because of the way she was feeling because she didn't understand the illness. I used to phone my sisters after a visit, and we would check in with how it went. At other times, Mum seemed to be settled in the home and more accepting of where she was, but we could never predict how she would be on any day. I used to be apprehensive on the way to see her and depending how it went I could go home feeling relieved that she was okay, or I'd go home in tears. Dementia was taking Mum away from us and I would watch her and see that far away expression in her face. She knew something was terribly wrong, but she couldn't understand what it was.

My mum had been a Christian for many years and on a Sunday night they would have someone from one of the local churches come in and have a time of singing and keeping people company. Mum loved that and for her it was like her church meeting. She had friends from her local church where she had been a member for several years, West Circular Road Baptist church had been her spiritual home and she had loved going there. Now the people came to her and she enjoyed those visits although they understood the times when Mum would be confused in her conversation. They were also sad that she was ill, and we all knew the outcome of dementia, so it was difficult for them too.

As Mum settled into care, we arranged her room to be as comfortable as possible for her. She had her books, her bible and pens and notebooks. Mum loved to underline scriptures in her bible and one of her favourite verses was in Isaiah

Isaiah 46:3-4

'I have cared for you since you were born. Yes, I carried you before you were born. I will be your God throughout

your lifetime – until your hair is white with age. I have made you and I will care for you. I will carry you along and save you.'

I realised that Mum was on a journey and that her life would end here, but God would never leave her. He cared for her and he was the one carrying her through this.

We sorted Mum's wardrobe with things we knew she liked, and her shoes, dresses and coats occupied every available inch of space. Mum liked her drinks cold so we got her a small fridge, the kind you would have in a caravan and she kept her soft drinks chilled until she wanted them. Her sweetie drawer was full with all sorts of goodies in there including her biscuits. However, sometimes she gave things away to other residents and then she thought we hadn't brought her anything. A quick visit to the garage across the road and we stockpiled the drawer again!

There was a care worker in the home that Mum was fond of and he had a great sense of humour and could make her laugh, well, most of the time. I went to see her one day and he had just come down from her room and he was smiling. He had gone into her room and she still hadn't decided what she wanted to wear that day so he took a lovely dress out of her wardrobe and told her that it would be nice on her. Unfortunately, Mum wasn't in a good mood that day so she told him if he liked it that much then he could wear it! I knew I might be in for a difficult visit.

While there were times when I was able to laugh at situations, there were times when I was upset leaving Mum. I used to go home, and my husband knew when I wanted to be on my own because I always went and had a bath.

It was here I would cry for Mum. I felt as though I was grieving for my Mum, yet she wasn't dead. I was grieving for the woman that she used to be, the one that I knew could look after herself and live independently. I grieved for the Mum that I used to go into town with or visit the Pancake House for cherry pancakes and fresh cream. I grieved because my mum didn't know herself anymore and that broke my heart. I cried because Mum was very much alive, but she was no longer the Mum we all knew. When I prayed, I asked for the strength and the grace to understand the journey she was now on. She still read her bible and talked about God, although she could be giving you a telling off the next minute. I knew without any doubt that Mum had faith and had a relationship with the Lord and at times when I visited her, I would sing a song she knew and she would join in or she would tell me to be quiet.

I needed to learn the best way to handle each visit with her. I also prayed this journey she was now on wouldn't last for years; I didn't want that for her. I loved Mum and to see the way in which this illness was affecting her was unbearable. I could visit her one day and my sister would go the next day and she would tell her she hadn't seen me, and she believed that because dementia was stealing her memory. It made me sad and it made me angry to watch this unfolding and yet I was grateful for the days when she seemed more like herself. However, those days were becoming fewer and far between. There were days when I would visit and she would ask when her Mum was coming to see her, or that she had seen her Dad. At first, I would try to reason with her that she was a bit confused and her Mum couldn't come to visit but in time I learnt to agree with whatever she said, because it wouldn't make any difference to her. In that moment she believed she saw her Dad and that was all that mattered. As she became more confused, she would become agitated and cry, it was so distressing to see her like this. Once she remembered she had a house and she wanted to go home so much that she got the opportunity to escape from the home.

She watched the door and waited and slipped out when the staff were busy. Immediately she was missed, and all the staff were looking for her and the family was informed she was out somewhere. Mum managed to get down the road but in her confused state she didn't know where she was. A staff member caught up with her and she said she was trying to get home, but she was lost. She was very distressed, and it took a long time for her to settle. Her mood was low for a few days and she was angry with everyone that she couldn't go home. I found this heart-breaking to watch because mum really couldn't understand that it wasn't safe for her to be on her own and she didn't realise just how ill she was. Dementia is frustrating for the person suffering from it and for the family to watch.

I noticed other residents in the home and while quite a few had regular visitors, there were those who didn't. It made me wonder how someone could live their life, have a marriage and a family yet come to be in care with no visitors at all. It was sad to witness this and yet it wasn't unusual for the staff to see this time and time again. I used to chat with people in the day room and I wondered what pain lay behind their smile. They seemed to accept their situation and made peace with it, but it would upset me to see elderly people who probably couldn't have foreseen the circumstances they found themselves in that led to them being in care. I could also see the distress of other families who like mine found themselves with a loved one suffering and unable to be taken care off at home. Visits were happy times, but I could see the suffering when it was time for them to leave. I always tried to make my visits with mum happy and positive and when she was in good form it was great but even when her mood was low, I'd still chat and smile and try to make it easy for her. As soon as I got home, I'd have a bath and cry.

Mum began to deteriorate with time, and she became more confused and her mood was low. None of the family could predict what way she would be when we visited, and I used to feel so sad.

It was like the Mum that I knew was fading away and there was nothing nobody could do to help her. She would still read her bible and I believed that in her spirit she knew her relationship with God and regardless of what was happening to her mind and her body, she still had her faith. In her confusion, she would talk to me about her parents and the time when she worked in the Blackstaff Mill on the Springfield Road. She remembered years later that she worked in the bakery shops on the Shankill Road and in Highfield Estate, but she couldn't remember who had come to visit her the day before. When I asked her, she would say that no one came, and she was on her own. It was sad that she couldn't remember her family from the day before.

I saw Mum becoming weary with each visit. Sometimes she would look at me and she seemed frightened and unable to comprehend why she was in this place that wasn't her house. The worst day for me came when I went to visit her, and she was talking to a member of staff when I arrived, and she introduced me as her sister. Instead of just agreeing with her like I normally would, I told her I was her daughter and she looked puzzled. She didn't know she had daughters. Another day I arrived and went into her room and she thought I worked there and I had to tell her I was her daughter and when I said my name, I could see the recognition in her eyes and then she smiled. I found these visits so difficult. My mum didn't always know who I was. As the illness progressed, I grieved inside, and it was so painful. I'd lost my Mum and she had become this frightened, confused woman who was weary with life. I began to pray that her time on earth would be short. I didn't want her to suffer anymore and my heart broke for her. I hated what dementia was doing to her and I knew from the staff that she spent more time on her own now. She didn't want to go to the day room to socialise and she was withdrawing more and more into herself.

The time had come for the family home to be given up as it was a rented house and when it was confirmed that mum could never live there again, the house had to be cleared out. My family found this distressing and just being in the house and going through Mum's belongings was so painful.

All the furniture was cleared out and clothes given to charity. We then cleaned the house from the top to the bottom until it was spotless and empty. On the day, my sister was going to give the keys back, she and I went over the house one last time. We sat on the carpet in the living room and shared some memories and we laughed. We knew we had to go out the front door one last time and we were avoiding it. Finally, we went into the hallway and had a quick look around and opened the front door. Walking out into the path, Sharon shut the door for the last time, and it broke our hearts. Another chapter in Mum's life was over and she wasn't here to witness it.

When I went home that day, I cried because I always thought that the time would come when Mum would die and then we would sort her house. I never realised that she would be in care and the house would go before her.

The next time I went to visit, she was in good form and as I smiled and chatted, I was thankful that she wasn't aware the home she had lived in for many years was gone. She didn't need to know.

March and April brought Mother's Day and Mum's birthday. As a family we did all we could to make it a happy time for her. Mum turned eighty and a month after that I had my fiftieth. I'd also written a novel and it was published. Mum used to keep a copy in her handbag, and she carried it everywhere and when one of the staff asked if they could borrow the book, she said no but they could look at the cover! Mum had always encouraged me with writing, and I was so glad I got a book published and she could see it.

I bought mum a lovely pink dress with a pearl necklace for her birthday and she loved it. She then put it in her wardrobe and didn't wear it, but she knew it was there. For a few weeks after my birthday in May, mum seemed brighter. When I visited her, we would sit outside in the sun and she enjoyed that. I noticed she was at peace and she laughed more. She still didn't always know who we all were but there was less pressure.

At the end of June, Mum became unwell. She had an infection and she was in bed when my sister Ruth and I visited. The doctor had been, and she was on antibiotics and she drifted in and out of sleep. I began to sing to her and even in her state of mind and physical illness, she lifted her hands to praise the Lord as I sang. As the day wore on, she got worse and was losing consciousness. An ambulance was called, and mum wasn't even aware of being taken out of the home. It seemed like she had a stroke. I wondered if she would come through it. At the hospital Mum had a scan that showed she had had a bleed on her brain. Over the next two days she went from sleeping to shouting out in her sleep. As I sat with her, I wondered what was happening to her. She never opened her eyes. On Sunday 4 July 2004, I went down to the hospital on the Sunday morning and stayed with her.

She slept quietly and I talked to her, I was convinced she could still hear. Other family members arrived as the day went on and Mum quietly slept. In the evening, my sisters and I and my aunt Kathleen were still with her, there had been no change. We were told to go home, and the staff would phone if any changes occurred. We kissed Mum and left. I was home less than thirty minutes when my sister phoned, we needed to get back to the hospital. When we arrived, we were told that shortly after we left, the nurse went in to check on mum and she stopped breathing. I wondered if this was the way Mum would have wanted it to be. She quietly slipped away and went home to be with the Lord. I had this picture in my mind of mum arriving in heaven and seeing loved ones who had gone before her and I wept.

I was happy for her but sad for myself and the family, yet I wouldn't wish her back. Besides, she wouldn't want to come. The battle with dementia was finally over for her and there was a sense of relief, yet I was heartbroken. The feeling of loss now that both my parents were gone was immense. I knew my life would be different without them and I grieved for them both.

My parents had reached the destination of the Christian life, and they were together with other loved ones and most of all, they had met Jesus Christ, now that's a picture to behold! Mum died on 4th July, when Independence Day is celebrated in the United States. I smiled when I realised that she was now independent of this world and in a place where this world was irrelevant now for her. She was in heaven and she was home.

The family began to plan her funeral and I remembered the pink dress with the pearl necklace I had bought her, she had never worn it, so we decided she would wear it with her white cardigan in death. When I went to see her in her coffin, she looked lovely. There was no trace of illness in her face and she was at peace and her dress was lovely. I didn't realise the day I bought the dress that it would be chosen for her in death, I was glad I'd bought it.

Mum's funeral was on the 7th July and lots of people came to her funeral. I tend to go through a funeral in a daze, it's like I'm there but it's not quite real. I remember it was a sunny day and as we laid Mum to rest, I knew the next time I saw her and my dad would be when I go to heaven but for now I had to learn to move on without them.

During the time my Mum was in care our family visited regularly every week. My brother Bobby and my sister-in-law Jeannie went every Sunday to see Mum as they both worked full time and lived further away. They would take Mum out for a drive and stop somewhere for ice cream which she loved. As mum's illness with dementia progressed, she didn't realise that Bobby and Jeanie were also going through a stressful time.

Their son Jim had been diagnosed with testicular cancer and he had been battling this for a long time. In March 2004, Jim was told he couldn't have any more treatment as the cancer had spread. His family were devastated. Over the next few months Jim's condition continued to deteriorate and he was moved to a hospice. His family were going through so much distress, yet Bobby and Jeannie never missed a visit to see mum. When mum died they were there to help plan her funeral and then they left to go and spend time with their son.

The day after mum's funeral, 8th July, Jim died, aged thirty-eight. His parents and family were heartbroken and so was the rest of the family. It's hard to lose someone as young as Jim and harder still for his parents. No parent wants to bury their child. They were totally heartbroken. We went to Jim's funeral on Saturday 10th July and I was so sad for his family. Nothing I could say would ease their pain, they had lost their child and their hearts were broken. No words can ever describe the pain they were going through. When the funeral was over, they would have to find their way through their grief. How does a parent even do that? When you feel that your heart has been torn from you and there is nothing but raw, ragged pain, how do you face another day? Bobby and Jeannie have an amazing marriage, they are a team and always have been and now, more than ever they would pull together as they came to accept that the son they loved so much had gone.

My one consolation and comfort was that my mum died a few days before Jim, and in my mind, she was waiting for him. God took her home before him so she would be there when he arrived. Our family had experienced two funerals in one week and the grief was so raw. As for Bobby and Jeanie, their grief was beyond words and their family were devastated. The days ahead would be difficult for each of us in different ways, but the one thing remaining was the knowledge that two people we loved were gone. How do we move on from that?

I look back on that time as one of the most painful in my life and I did what I always do, I turned to God, who would be my strength every day and my comfort when I cried.

Psalm 34:18-19

The Lord is close to the broken-hearted; he rescues those whose spirits are crushed. The righteous person faces many troubles, but the Lord comes to the rescue each time.

Chapter 10

Following Mum's death, we had to clear out her room in the care home. It was upsetting going through her things, yet it was necessary. I picked up a bottle of perfume and sprayed it and it was like she was there. Her clothes, books and family photos were packed up and the room was left clean and tidy for whoever would move in after her. The staff at the home had been so good to Mum and incredibly supportive of the family. Leaving there was like closing the door on another chapter in our lives and it was sad. Everything was done that had to be done and now we had to begin to move on with our lives.

I felt empty inside now both my parents were gone. Something that had once felt so familiar no longer existed. The family connection we had with them was gone. I went up to the cemetery and saw Mum's name had been put on the headstone just below Dad's.

The realisation that they were gone was heart-breaking and the feeling of loss was overwhelming. I know that death is part of life but it's only when both my parents had died that I experienced that sense of the family circle being broken. It was so difficult to accept. I had times when I would begin my day thinking I was going to see Mum and then remembering she was gone. When I went into town I would look over to where I'd get the bus to Mum's, but I wouldn't be doing that anymore. I'd had this routine where I'd do some shopping and get something nice for lunch and then get on the bus to head to her house. I'd fight back tears as I walked along the street because I felt so sad.

Learning to move on after Mum's death was hard. So many times, I'd forget she was no longer here, and I'd pick up the phone to call her house. I'd done that a lot when she was in care but even so, it was an automatic thing when I thought of something I would normally say to her, I'd get the thought, I must phone Mum. Every day my mind would replay memories of my life with her, some good and some not so good. I experienced such a void inside me and I'd cry all the time. When I was younger and both my parents were alive, it was easier to think of death being part of life because it had not affected me. With both my parents gone, I now experienced the pain of grief and the emptiness inside and sometimes I just didn't know how to get a day without crying.

After a time, I began to find acceptance and I began to realise that my parents had lived a long life, and this was their time to be at rest and at peace. When I visited their grave there was still that part of me that grieved yet I accepted that it was okay to grieve. It was okay to cry and miss them. With the passing of time I began to heal inside, and my memories became sweeter and I'd smile instead of crying.

The first year after Mum died was the hardest. Anniversaries are difficult occasions. The first Christmas was sad, but I took a wreath up to the grave for her and Dad. The first Mother's Day was hard because I no longer had to go into a shop for a card and when I looked at all the cards on display, I missed Mum so much. Her birthday was the following month and soon after was the anniversary of her death.

All those first times are hard and I'm not sure that time is a great healer, I think I just became more accepting.

The seasons of life come and go and will continue to do so and the learning comes in whatever season I find myself in. It is bittersweet at times. Sometimes I have asked the Lord why life is so painful, and I realise that when you love someone then it's going to hurt when they are gone. That love in my heart is always there and I have memories stored away in my mind that I sometimes recall with pleasure and sometimes with tears. It's life and my greatest learning curve is continuing to live the rest of my life as best I can and live in relationship with the Lord every day. I find my peace in knowing that my parents are in heaven and that one day I will see them again. They have lived their lives and in life they had their share of troubles and hard times, but, no more. I smile at the idea of mum and dad getting along in heaven, now that will be a sight to behold!

Revelation 7:17

For the Lamb on the throne will be their Shepherd. He will lead them to springs of life-giving water. And God shall wipe every tear from their eyes.

Chapter 11

Through the seasons of my life since 1998 I have had to learn to deal with fibromyalgia daily. There is a lot of information available about this condition. The internet is flooded with articles and websites and there are a lot of books on the subject. I can only speak from my own personal experience.

In 1997 I had an accident and fell down a flight of concrete steps. I hurt my back and after being seen at the hospital I was referred to physiotherapy. This eased the pain for a time, but I began to experience pain down my legs and then my upper body was affected. Over a period of a year I had several tests done and a scan. I then saw a consultant at Musgrave Hospital who confirmed I had fibromyalgia. When my doctor first mentioned to me that I had fibromyalgia, I was puzzled, because I'd never even heard the word before. I then assumed it was something I'd get a prescription for and it would go away! I was so naïve. Then he said I might have to give up my job because there was no cure for this illness. I loved my work and I had no intention of giving it up. Yet, within a year, that's exactly what happened.

Within a short time of losing my job, I then gave up my studies with Open University and then the depression hit. It took me a while to realise that I was grieving for the career that I thought I was going to have and the degree that I was working hard towards. My work and my education became another loss in my life, and I didn't know how to cope with it. I didn't understand the full implications of having fibromyalgia and I'd also suffered injury to my lower spine.

I have heard fibromyalgia called a disease, a condition, an illness and a disability. For me, it is an illness that affects my mobility and my mental and emotional health. Physically, I experience pain every day and at night. The pain can be on different levels and no two days are the same with fibromyalgia. I face a daily battle with pain and fatigue and when I talk to people about this, I tend to focus on those two symptoms. The truth is, there are a lot of symptoms and I find it difficult to discuss them. It is a deceptive illness. I say this because, I can look alright and if I have a little makeup on, no one will know there was anything wrong with me. I also try awfully hard to appear normal, whatever normal is! My sleep is affected, in that, I wake up after a few hours, usually because of pain, and that means getting up and taking medication and a hot drink and eventually I'll sleep again for a few hours. Even with medication I don't always have a deep restful sleep. Fatigue is one of the worst symptoms, because I sometimes feel like I've been hit by an oncoming train! I have little energy and on a good day, if I make it into the shower, then that feels like an achievement. I get that feeling of achievement like I used to get when I'd had a good day at work. Only now, that sense of doing something well was down to being able to have a shower and put on clean pyjamas. I can be out of bed and within an hour, it's like I haven't had any sleep and I can go back to bed. 'Fibro fog' is another symptom that really gets me! It's when my brain feels like cotton wool. I can't think straight, and I find it difficult to make the simplest decisions. I also do silly things, which my grandsons find very funny. For example, I recently went to put on the washing machine and discovered there were no clothes in it, yet I knew I had got the washing from the laundry basket a short time earlier.

I traced my steps back to the bedroom, but I hadn't left it there, then I went and looked in the laundry basket, but it was empty. Now I was puzzled. How could I possible lose my washing? I eventually found it. Next to the washing machine is a swing top bin for rubbish and I'd put the washing in the bin! I couldn't remember doing this. Another example was last Christmas, I had settled to watch television and I turned on the sky box, but the television hadn't come on and I thought something had gone wrong with it. Turns out I was pointing the tv remote at the Christmas tree! I have times when I'm truly thankful that God looks after me, because I don't always do a good job of looking after myself.

When I do silly things, I make a joke about it but, this is a part of my life now. No two days are the same and I never know what a day will bring with this illness. Depression is another ongoing battle and I get times when I just shut down and rest because I don't have the physical or mental capacity to battle it. Other times I can focus on reading or writing, and it helps to bring me through the mental battle and the physical pain.

I no longer make long term plans, because I usually have to cancel and then I feel bad. It's much easier to say no to things and in that way, I don't disappoint other people or myself. When I do plan to go out, say, to church, I prepare from the day before. I leave out my clothes, shoes, jewellery and I know which coat and bag I'll take. However, even after the preparations I don't always get out. I can have a restless night when the pain flares and by the time I should be getting up, I'm ready to go to sleep. I used to get disappointed with myself when this happened but now, I accept that it is what it is and maybe next time I'll get out.

I have been on various medications for years and I'm thankful I have access to them. I've gone through periods of physio, spinal injections and acupuncture. All of these do help, but there is no one treatment that will take away the symptoms.

It has taken years for me to learn that it's all about pain management. Depression is handled with antidepressants and I've been on so many different ones. They do help with nerve pain and sleep but sometimes there are side effects that are worse than the illness. Depression can hit when I least expect it. Usually if I've had a flare up of pain and fatigue. I struggle with daily life in general and then it's like I wake up one morning and this dark curtain is across my mind and I can't move it. Rest and reading help me through and I like to write. Emotionally, it's a battle that seems unending. I can go from my positive self, then swing to negative and then I get to the point where I don't want to go on like this anymore. Of course, I do!

This is where the rubber hits the road I suppose. This is where faith comes in and when I talk about faith, I don't mean some kind of wishy-washy belief in God. No, I'm talking, up close and personal with Jesus. I know what it's like to pray through the pain when no medication is helping. I play CDs, I sing and I worship and other times I am just quiet. In the stillness with God I learn to trust him to bring me out the other side of this. I find that in being quiet, I receive grace and rest to face another day. For twenty years I have battled with this illness and I've prayed about it many times. I've also been prayed for several times and I'm thankful for the strength I receive because of prayer. However, there have been times when I have questioned God as to why I still battle with this horrible illness that affects so many areas of my life. I've also come up against the well-meaning advice and opinions of others. Let me be clear, people have had the best of intentions and never would intentionally hurt me, but at times that's exactly what has happened. Over the years when I've been prayed for and then I'm still in pain the following week, I've been asked where my faith is? I've been questioned about hidden sin in my life that might block my healing and I've been told to just walk it out!

I know in my heart that people really do mean well, however, I've spent so much time questioning myself and examining myself for secret sins until I'm on a guilt trip because I've been prayed for but I'm in pain. I've questioned my relationship with the Lord and my level of faith. I wonder if there is something about me that is stuck and can't move on in this glorious healing I'm yearning for. You know, when my mind goes on that merry-go-round of endless questions and doubts, then I run to my Father.

Psalm 91:1-2

'Those who live in the shelter of the Most High will find rest in the shadow of the Almighty. This I declare about the Lord; He alone is my refuge, my place of safety; he is my God and I trust him.'

I don't have all the answers as to why things have happened to me. I do know that God is my place of safety, he is the One that I lean on when times are difficult. Many years ago, when I first became a Christian there was the belief that if you were suffering then God was trying to teach you something, and way back then I believed it. However, I must have been a slow learner because it has taken years for me to realise that a loving parent doesn't treat his child in that way!

My God is a loving Father, he is my Father and His Son Jesus is Lord in my life. A loving Father doesn't hurt his children in order to teach them. That teaching damaged me for years. Let me explain. I grew up as a child in churches and I picked up a lot of information.

Somewhere along the way I really did think of God being someone who loved me but if I stepped out of line then he was waiting with the big stick. I felt I had to always walk the straight line or I'd be in big trouble.

The enemy sold me the lie, that I wasn't good enough and I was bad. Lies are the opposite of what God has to say about me. Deception is the enemy's favourite tool to attack the mind and subconsciously I believed that I must be doing something wrong if I was suffering. I didn't feel secure in a loving relationship with God all the time because I was still wary of him. My breakthrough moment came when as an adult I was praying in my room and I began to address God as 'DaddyGod', but I felt uncomfortable. I stopped praying and sat still. I couldn't understand why I was unable to get past this. In being still and worshipping, God showed me a picture of me when I was a little girl and as a child, I knew God was real, but I was hiding behind a door and didn't want to come out. I was afraid. In that moment I felt like a little girl, hiding from her Father and I began to cry. I wanted to experience the love he had for me without being afraid of him. The next picture I saw was of me as an adult but with the heart of a child. I ran into what appeared to be a study. There was a desk and I could smell beautiful polish and there was a big leather chair. Seated on the chair was 'DaddyGod' and I ran and jumped up on his lap. He embraced me close to him and it felt like the most natural thing in my life to be close to him. In my heart I experienced the change inside as I worshipped. Emotionally I was set free from the lies I had believed and now I know what it's like to love my Father as 'Daddy' and sometimes I even like Papa.

Galatians 4:4-7

'But when the right time came, God sent his Son, born of a woman, subject to the law, God sent him to buy freedom for us who were slaves to the law, so that he could adopt us as his very own children. And because we are his children, God sent the Spirit of his Son into our hearts, prompting us to call out, 'Abba Father.' Now you are no longer a slave but God's own child, God has made you an heir.'

My identity is in God, I'm his child and I have learnt over the years that the things I don't understand, or I don't have all the answers to, then I must trust him that he knows the answers. When he wants me to know then he will tell me. For now, I accept I have challenges with my health, but those challenges do not define me.

Every day, I learn to overcome the challenges I face. I have particularly good days where I achieve a lot and I have days when having a shower and resting is also an achievement. I believe what is said in *Isaiah 53:5;* by his stripes I am healed and when he said, it is finished, he meant it! In him I find my healing and whether that healing is manifest now in this life or the next, the point is, I have healed. Praise God, there is no pain in heaven.

We live in a broken world but thankfully it won't always be like this. Jesus Christ will one day return to earth and set up his Kingdom and the things we struggle with now will be forgotten.

My God is a good God and his plan for me is healing. I believe him and I've his protection, blessing and favour in my life. My faith is my shield and deep inside me my foundation is relationship with Jesus. He is the rock I build my life upon. In him is my trust.

Psalm 13:5-6

But I trust in your unfailing love. I will rejoice because you have rescued me. I will sing to the Lord because he is good to me.

Chapter 12

In 2006 as I continued to look after my health with pain management I decided to learn to drive. Now I'd done my test several times in years gone by and I failed. I was content for a time with my husband driving me anywhere I wanted to go but there was a part of me longed to be able to drive myself. I imagined going shopping in my own little car and I liked the idea of being more independent. I'd experienced several falls when I'd gone out on my own and there was pain in my legs. I prayed about it and I felt this strong urge to start driving lessons and this time I would pass my test. Usually when I pray about something, I wait a while before doing anything about it. However, I felt compelled to book my lessons. I believed this really was something I had to do.

I told my husband I was going back to driving and he smiled as if to say here we go again. He knew how upset I used to be when I'd failed my test but when he saw I really wanted to do it, he told me to go for it. I was fifty-one when I began my lessons in May and I was fifty-two in September when I passed my test. I was so happy. I felt like I'd conquered the world!

I shared the car with my husband but eventually I got my own car and I loved it. Even now when I'm out driving, I don't take it for granted. This was like my biggest achievement ever.

At the end of October, I fell in the house. I was running up the stairs and I tripped and went down on my left hand. I heard the bone break and then the pain kicked in. It was a Saturday night and going to A&E was the last place I wanted to be.

Billy took me to hospital, and we were there for hours. During the waiting time to see the doctor, I was sent to triage and Billy came with me. My hand had swollen by this time and I knew it was broken because I heard it happen. I was then told that my wedding ring would have to be cut off and I was so upset. As the nurse began to cut the ring I began to cry. Billy kept telling me he would buy me a new ring but that wasn't the reason I was crying. Deep inside I felt that as the ring was being cut there was a separation inside me, I didn't understand it, but the feeling of loss was real. Eventually the ring was off, and I had x-rays done and my hand put in plaster. It was after 2am when we got home, and I was in pain and exhausted. I went to bed and Billy stayed up to watch television. As I drifted off to sleep, I remembered that feeling of loss I'd had when my wedding ring was being cut off, and it disturbed me. It was a thought I would keep on my heart for a later time. With my hand in plaster I couldn't drive for weeks and I was so frustrated! Thankfully, the bone healed and within two months I was driving again. Happiness reigned supreme!

Christmas was fast approaching, and I loved being able to go shopping for the family and load the car up with pressies. The week before Christmas, Billy and I went up to Carmoney cemetery and put Christmas wreaths on family graves, his dad and sister and my parents. I used to get the wreaths made especially and it was just a thoughtful thing we liked to do together. I missed my parents at this time and liked to put a nice wreath with a little robin on their grave.

The week leading up to Christmas we did the food shopping which Billy loved. He put all sorts into the trolley and the bill was always much higher when he came with me. There was a butcher's shop in town that a friend of his owned and Billy always ordered our turkey and other meat there and we just had to collect it.

He always made vegetable soup and where I would buy cut vegetables, Billy liked to buy vegetables and cut his own. He made lovely soup. On Christmas Eve the kitchen was filled with lovely smells of the turkey cooking and freshly made soup. Before we went to bed, we would open one present each. I was like an excited child.

On Christmas morning we came downstairs and I'd put the kettle on and then we opened our presents. I loved it. Eventually when we were ready to go out, we went to visit family. It was a lovely mild day that Christmas and it was perfect. We had dinner with family and saw our grandchildren and it was such a good day. When we were at our daughter's house there were presents under the tree and there was an extra one for me. I opened the gift bag and inside was a silver box. When I opened it, I was delighted at the jewellery inside. There was a necklace, earrings and bracelet and a card with love from Billy. I was delighted with the surprise. I remember that day as being so special in every way.

When we got home, the first thing I did was take my makeup off and put on my new pyjamas. Billy made lovely snacks for us and a glass of chilled wine. The house was warm and cosy, and the Christmas tree lights twinkled. I curled up on the sofa and we watched television although sometimes we fell asleep! I remember every detail of Christmas 2006 because it was perfect. There was one thing that caused concern. Billy had been in the kitchen making a late-night snack and suddenly he felt as though an electric shock had gone down his left arm. He woke up on the kitchen floor and he had no idea what had happened. When he got up, he felt fine, but it puzzled both of us although it didn't happen again.

New Year 2007 we celebrated quietly at home. Billy had cooked a lovely dinner and we had a relaxing night. I always went to bed before him because I liked to read, whereas Billy would stay up to watch television. I remember kissing him goodnight and feeling very content as I went to bed. Our marriage had been through horrendous times over the years, but we had survived, and we had got to that place of acceptance with each other.

Gone were the level of expectations that neither of us could deliver on. It had taken years to get here but I was so glad we had. A new year lay ahead, and Billy was already talking of selling the small boat and getting a bigger boat. He also suggested that we sell our house and buy a houseboat! No Billy was my response. I like my home comforts. We had got the house decorated and it was looking good, but I know if I had agreed to the houseboat idea, Billy would have done it!

I went to bed and left him to think about the boat he wanted to buy. I had a new book I wanted to start reading and along with my tea and chocolate I was happy. It felt good to be at this place of contentment and our Christmas and New year had been perfect. I was grateful for all I had in my life.

Philippians 4:4-7

Always be full of joy in the Lord. I say it again – rejoice! Let everyone see that you are considerate in all you do. Remember, the Lord is coming soon. Don't worry about anything; instead, pray about everything. Tell God what you need and thank him for all he has done. Then you will experience God's peace, which exceeds anything we can understand. His peace will guard your hearts and minds as you live in Christ Jesus.

Chapter 13

January was wet and cold, and Billy worked in a job where he started early. An outdoor job was great in the summer, but he didn't like it in winter. An opportunity arose for a new job which involved teaching young people a trade in white goods. For many years Billy worked at repairing washing machines and cookers etc. He was more than qualified to apply for this job. He got an interview and shortly after he got the job. He was happy to get back to doing the job he loved. The salary was better, and it was near home so I used to drive him to work while we were still sharing the car and then I could go shopping. I loved that!

In February, Billy got the flu. Now it was unusual for Billy to be ill. He just didn't get sick. I got him the usual flu remedies, but nothing helped. Billy also tried his own remedies, as in a hot whiskey, at least he slept.

He was loving his new job and he would never take time off, but I knew he was ill. His appetite wasn't good and yet he loved his food and I could tell this was getting him down. I made an appointment with the doctor and I went with him, just to make sure he went. Billy rarely saw the doctor and he wasn't comfortable with it. He was told it was a virus and it would clear eventually. A few nights later he woke up with a cough and he had a fever and was sweating badly. I was worried. The next day was Saturday so we went to the out of hours Doctor who examined him, but they sent us over to the Mater hospital. Billy had an x-ray and we then saw the doctor. We were told he had pneumonia and he was put onto antibiotics for two weeks. He took the medication, but he still wasn't well, and his appetite hadn't improved.

We went back to the hospital and Billy had another x-ray. We expected it to be clear and we were surprised when we were told there was still an infection in his lungs. He was given stronger antibiotics and told to come back in two weeks. Throughout this illness, Billy never took one day off work. He loved his new job and he had settled quickly into it. He loved teaching people a trade that would benefit them in gaining employment.

We went back to the hospital two weeks later and Billy had another x-ray, but the doctor was still concerned about the infection and said he would refer Billy to a consultant. At that time, I was attending the outpatient clinic at the hospital, so I phoned my consultant's secretary and explained the situation with Billy and thankfully he had an appointment within two weeks.

On Wednesday 25th April 2007, we had an appointment with the consultant at the Mater Hospital. We saw Dr Kidney at the chest clinic, he is a lung specialist. Billy had routine tests done and then he had an x-ray done. We waited for the results and then saw the consultant. He was concerned with the x-ray. He said this would be treated as urgent! An appointment was made for a Bronchoscopy at Belfast City Hospital for Tuesday 1st May, followed by a CT scan at the Mater Hospital on Tuesday 8th May and then a PET scan at the Royal Hospital on Wednesday 9th May. It was a terribly busy week!

The Bronchoscopy involved a camera being inserted into Billy's lungs and thankfully, he was sedated for this. Julie went with us and she and I went and had a coffee while the test was being done.

Billy went to recovery afterwards and when he woke up, we were able to see him. After a few minutes, the consultant came in and I just remember feeling so scared. He looked at Billy and then told him he had big trouble down there! There was a tumour in his left lung and the scans would tell us more. If Billy was worried, then he didn't show it. He just wanted further tests done so as we would know what exactly he was dealing with and what could be done about it. Even when we were on our own at home, he was the one reassuring me! The following week the scans were completed, and we waited for an appointment with the consultant for the results. Billy still had the attitude that we will wait and see what happens, but I knew he was worried. He was in a new job which he loved and while he had arranged time off to have tests done, he never missed a day off work.

On Thursday 17th May we saw the consultant at the Mater Hospital and we were anxious, and Billy was quiet. Sometimes we didn't need to speak, but we just knew what each other was feeling.

The consultant informed us that the scans confirmed the tumour and it was malignant. We discussed the possibility of surgery, which would be to remove part of his lung and then follow up treatment if necessary. We agreed to this. There was to be a meeting the next day with the surgical team at the City Hospital to discuss his condition. We would then get an appointment with a consultant at the City Hospital, hopefully to discuss a date for surgery. We didn't have to wait long for the appointment. Exactly a week later, on the 24th May, we were at the City Hospital to see the consultant.

Up to this point Billy and I felt that surgery would be the plan, maybe with follow up chemotherapy. We were both positive about this appointment and Billy had accepted that the next few weeks would be tough, but it would be worth it.

We went into the office and the Consultant was reading the medical notes. After the polite welcome, Billy asked him if a date had been set for the operation. The doctor then told us that an operation was no longer an option. The scans had shown a second tumour and the cancer had spread. Billy had non-small-cell carcinoma. There was silence for a few seconds. It felt like an explosion in my brain, as the doctor's words began to sink in. Billy and I grabbed each other's hands and held on. I felt so sick inside. It's that feeling of, I know what the doctor is saying, yet I can't quite believe it. Billy asked the doctor how long he had left. I could hear the words but, in my mind, I was screaming, no, this can't be happening. The doctor told us he had nine months to a year, and they wanted to begin treatment which would consist of chemotherapy and radiotherapy. Treatment would be palliative as the cancer had spread. The doctor's attitude was lovely as he explained the treatment and he realised we both had had a shock. Billy remained calm and talked to the doctor, but I couldn't speak. We left the office and Billy was taken for an x-ray. I went outside and stood in the fresh air. I couldn't cry, or even think. I was still in denial. In my heart I was praying, 'what now Lord?' Then I realised I just had to breathe, take in the fresh air and try to clear my head. Billy came out of the hospital and we walked towards the car in silence. The shock had hit. We sat in the car for a few minutes and held hands, then Billy being his positive self, tried to reassure me that treatment would help, and he might get longer. We were clinging to threads of hope.

The family were told that day and Billy tried to avoid some details. I think we both were in denial and if we didn't talk about it then it wouldn't seem real. It still felt like I was on the outside of something, looking in, and I didn't want to go there.

I realised that other people get news like this every day but today it was us who got the news and I didn't know how to cope with it. I was devastated.

I went for a drive later that day while Billy had a rest. He needed time on his own and my way of coping was to drive and pray in the car. I remembered not long after Billy and I got married, we were in town one day and an elderly couple were walking in front of us and she was holding onto his arm. They must have been in their eighties. Billy noticed them and turned to me and said that we would be like that couple and we would be old together and still out in the town. I laughed at him and he told me again, that would be us. I parked the car in a lay by and I cried. We thought we would have years ahead of us but that morning in the hospital, all those dreams had come crashing down. Billy was fifty-seven and he had been told he had terminal cancer. It didn't get any worse than that.

As I prayed in the car, I was aware of knowing that there is peace in the storm. I felt surrounded by the presence of the Lord, and I drew strength from him. This would be the way I would cope with every day. God would be my strength and then I would be able to care for Billy. I still faced my own health problems every day and while they paled in comparison to cancer, I still needed the strength to look after myself if I were to look after Billy. For now, we would cope with day to day life, but there would be challenges as time went on.

Driving home, I thought back to early that morning when we were getting ready to go to the hospital, how positive Billy had been. Now I felt our world had been turned upside down and everything we thought we knew about life had changed. Nothing would be the same from this day. Long term plans would-be put-on hold because we didn't know exactly how long we would have together. It's like, life comes to a standstill and we were left thinking, what now?

Billy was quiet when I got home and still had the attitude that treatment would be a help and then we would see after that. I didn't feel that way, but I wouldn't say it. I knew that treatment would help but there would be no let's wait and see, we had been told the cancer was terminal. Now we waited on Billy's first appointment for chemotherapy at the cancer centre at Belfast City Hospital.

Nahum 1:7

The Lord is good, a strong refuge when trouble comes. He is close to those who trust him.

Chapter 14

The month of May wasn't all bad news. For several years Billy had a small boat which we used every summer. However, his dream was to have a cabin cruiser since we had decided against a houseboat! He found the one he wanted on the internet and it was in England. He and Colin went across to have a look at it and Billy loved it. It needed some TLC, but Billy bought it before it was sent to auction. They arranged to have the boat brought over to Northern Ireland and it was to be berthed in the Moorings, a marina in Enniskillen. The Moorings overlooked Lough Erne and it is such a beautiful place. Colin arranged for the boat to be painted and the name of the boat put on it. Billy had a long think over what to call the boat. He decided to call it New Beginnings because he had rescued it from it from the auction and given it a new beginning and it was also a new boat for the family, and we would have lots of new memories to make. When the boat was ready, we were excited going down to see it. It was my first time at the Moorings and as I stood overlooking Lough Erne I was overwhelmed by the beauty and the peace that surrounded me.

The boat was beautiful, painted white with a jade green canopy and the sign writing of the name of the boat was also green. It was awesome. Colin had got a captain's hat for Billy with his name on it, so he was well pleased. Before we went out on the Lough, we had to christen the boat. We had champagne and Colin shook the bottle, so it sprayed over the boat and we clapped. We took photos and laughed, and we were happy. Sailing out of the marina and down the

Lough was awesome. The sun was shining and warm, I loved the breeze in my face and the spray of the water. Julie and the boys loved it and the boys wanted to learn how to drive the boat too!

The first weekend on the boat was special for me because it was my birthday. We went to the restaurant at the Moorings for dinner that night and after we had eaten the staff brought in a birthday cake as the family sang happy birthday and the boys helped to blow out my candles. It had been such a happy day and it felt like a normal day in our lives. The next morning, we went out on the Lough and the sun shone. Colin and Julie had a try at mooring the boat, not entirely successfully but after a few attempts and a little bump, it was perfect.

The family went home later that day and Billy and I had another night on the boat. We hadn't spoken about the cancer or the treatment that lay ahead while the family were there. We sat on the deck enjoying the view of the lough, the sun setting and a gentle breeze. It was beautiful and peaceful and miles away from hospitals and treatments. These are the memories that I kept on my heart. Precious moments shared together, and I realised just how much every moment counts.

When I was at the boat I always slept well, and I felt rested. There was a stillness in my heart that I knew to be God and I was strengthened in my spirit. God knew exactly what lay ahead for us and I was aware of leaning in close to him in preparation for the days ahead.

We went home and mentally Billy was preparing himself for whatever lay ahead. He was to have his first chemo appointment on 30th May. As it was the first one, he had to be admitted overnight. We set off that morning with his bag and went to the Cancer Centre.

Arriving at the ward we were sent to the day room and a nurse then came in and took us through the procedure, then blood tests were taken. Our family called up to see how Billy was getting on and then he was admitted to the ward. He was pleased he had a room of his own. It didn't take long for the procedure to begin. Billy was to be given two chemotherapy drugs through an infusion in his arm. Gemcitabine and Cisplatin are used in the treatment of cancer and are anti-cancer drugs. They are given to destroy or control the cancer cells and to relieve the symptoms and shrink the tumour. Chemotherapy drugs destroy the cancer cells by damaging them so as they can't divide and grow. When these drugs are given, they enter the bloodstream and reach all parts of the body, this is called systemic treatment. These drugs can also cause damage to normal cells which are growing and dividing, and this may cause side effects. Billy was to have four cycles of chemotherapy and when he was admitted for the first one, he was feeling positive and his blood tests showed a normal white cell count so chemo could go ahead.

I stayed with Billy until after dinner. He was tired but there's something about being in hospital that made him feel tired anyway. It felt so strange leaving the hospital without him. This was the first time he had to stay overnight and when I drove away from the car park, it just didn't feel right coming home alone. I was tired and went to bed early. I phoned Billy to say good night and he said he was fine. I had a restless night despite being so tired. Early the next morning, the phone rang, and it was Billy. He was being discharged and he was ready to go.

I quickly got dressed and out to the car. I'd do breakfast when Billy was home. I arrived at the cancer centre and Billy was waiting outside with his bag, so I didn't have to park! We were both happy the first chemo session was over, and he was coming home. We stopped at a bakery along the way and got sausage rolls and cakes. Billy suddenly had an appetite and I was glad to see his mood had lightened.

Billy seemed to respond well to the chemo and the following week we went back to the hospital but this time to the day clinic. The Bridgewater Suite is based in the City Hospital and when we arrived the first thing to be done was blood tests. We were able to have coffee while we waited on the results and if his white cell count were ok, the chemo could go ahead. The good thing about the day clinic is being there for the treatment but being able to go home afterwards. Billy was usually tired after treatment and he would sleep for a couple of hours when we got home. It was after the second round of chemo that the side effects began to show. Billy was tired and had more pain, his appetite was poor, and he just felt unwell. He rested for a few days and began to feel better. The next week when we went back to the Bridgewater Suite for another round of Chemo, they took the usual blood tests as soon as we arrived. Billy still hadn't been feeling great and he wanted to get the treatment over and get home. Things didn't go according to plan that day. The blood test results showed there was a fall in his white cell count and his immune system was low. Chemo had to be put off for another week until he was stronger. Billy was annoyed at this, but this is where side effects can wipe out the good the chemo appears to be doing. We went home and he slept.

In learning to look after Billy, there were things I had to look out for. I'd encourage him with his eating and when he wanted to start drinking various juices, we bought a juicer and I sourced recipes that would help boost Billy's immune system. Basically, he could have wherever he liked when it came to food, if he were eating or juice drinking, I didn't mind. One of the side effects that he experienced was feeling the cold more. He always had a blanket over him as he slept in the recliner chair.

I had to be mindful about his temperature and if it was high then I had to phone the helpline at the Cancer Centre. If it went too low, I still had to phone. This happened after he was sent home and hadn't been able to get his chemo. I'd taken his temperature and it was up, he didn't feel well and hadn't eaten much that day. I phoned that night and left a message and within minutes I got a call back. I was told to bring Billy into hospital. When we arrived, it was after 11pm, and Billy was complaining about the cold, he couldn't get heat into his body. He was admitted onto the ward and had his own room and then blood tests were taken. While we waited for the results, the nurse brought him extra blankets for his bed, but he still shivered. I was distraught, although I didn't let him see it. He kept saying, he was so cold. In the end I got onto the bed and lay over him and held him so that my body heat would help him and eventually the shivering stopped. The blood test results showed that Billy had an infection, his immune system was low, and we had been told that this can be a side effect of the chemo. Now as I watched Billy experience it, I was worried about what lay ahead. Billy was put on antibiotics and he also had a blood transfusion. I stayed with him until 3am and then he fell asleep and I left. Driving home, I was upset, and I was again coming home without him. It had been a long night and I was exhausted. When I got home, I made tea and went up to bed. I was restless when Billy was out of the house and I worried about him. I missed him too and I didn't want to think of my future without him. I tried not to dwell on those thoughts. We had to face one day at a time and right now I needed a few hours' sleep.

Billy recovered and had another cycle of chemo at the Bridgewater Suite and he seemed to tolerate it well this time. When we weren't at the hospital, we went down to the boat. Being at Lough Erne was the one place we could all relax and be at peace. We never thought about cancer when we were there. Billy was always in a better mood and he slept well. It was like we were a normal couple again, in our own bubble.

When we got back, Billy had another overnight stay at the cancer centre, and we were used to the routine now. I would stay with him until nighttime and then I'd go home. It was at times like this I was so grateful I'd passed my driving test the year before. At least we didn't have to worry about transport! The next morning, I would wake up early and wait for Billy's phone call. I loved getting into the car and going over to the hospital for him. He would be standing outside the Cancer Centre with his bag as I drove in. I'd put the window down and say, 'Do you want a lift mate?' Then we would laugh as he got into the car. We headed to the bakery and got supplies and then home. After he had eaten, he liked to sleep in his chair. I got on with doing things around the house. I was glad to have him home.

Billy's next treatment was at the Bridgewater Suite at the City Hospital. He didn't mind going to the day clinic. The waiting was difficult for him sometimes as his treatment couldn't begin until we had the results of his blood tests. Then he would be taken to a treatment room where there would be several others seated in recliner chairs having their treatment. Billy would get comfortable and the chemo began. It took a long time and I'd get a blanket for him and he would sleep for a while. I would always have something to read and I'd sit with him while the treatment lasted. It was good when it was over, and we could leave. When we were at home, Billy would have something to eat and then he'd sleep. I knew I could phone the helpline if there were any problems. Throughout July and August, his treatment continued. There were side effects and the one thing that got him down was the tiredness. He slept a lot more but when he was feeling better, he would go down to the boat. Sometimes I went but not all the time. It was good for Billy and Colin to spend time together, another time it was Billy and Julie.

During the time when Billy went down to the boat without me, I went to church and I got a lot of love and support there.

Friends were praying for Billy and for our family as we went through this time. I also had time on my own with Billy out of the house but not in the hospital! I needed that time.

I would write in my journal, take time to pray and to read my bible. More than ever, I was aware of how ill Billy was and how uncertain our time together would be. When I was alone, I could cry when I needed to and by the time Billy arrived home, I was ready to look after him and I felt stronger within myself.

The summer days were warm, and Billy loved to get out of the house. We had a day trip with Julie and the boys to Ballycastle. We went into the park for the boys to play and Billy sat on the grass on the hill. I looked over at him and he was watching the boys and smiling. He rested for a while before we set off to Ballintoy. Billy loved to go into the café there and we had lunch and sat outside in the sun. I took a few pictures and I was aware that I was capturing memories. I didn't want that summer to end because I didn't know if we would get to do this again. Ballintoy Harbour was a special place for Billy and me.

The first year we were married, we went to Ballintoy and we were walking along the harbour when a boat came in.

There was a sign for boat trips, but Billy and I were the only two people waiting, and we didn't think they would take the boat out just for us. However, that's exactly what the skipper did. We went on board and sailed out of the harbour and up towards the rope bridge. It was lovely being out on the water and the sea breeze was refreshing. When we got back, we then had lunch in the café. It is one of those happy memories that will always stay with me.

Billy began the last cycle of chemo on the 8th August. He was admitted overnight to the cancer centre and by now we had gotten used to the routine. I stayed with him and then went home at night and early the next morning, Billy would be on the phone for me to come and get him. After having something to eat, he would sleep for a few hours. In the days that followed he experienced more side effects.

He was in considerable pain and a rash covered his back. He was prescribed antibiotics, but they had made him sick. On the 15th August we went to the day clinic at the Bridgewater Suite. His blood tests were taken and thankfully they were okay, and his chemo went ahead. He was also given a cream for the rash, which was a side effect of the chemo drugs. We were there for several hours but as this was his last chemo appointment, he was quite positive. We celebrated by stopping the bakery for his favourite chocolate cake on the way home.

That weekend Billy and Colin went down to the boat, but they came home on Sunday night. I noticed how tired Billy was and he was short of breath. I got him settled on the recliner chair with a blanket over him and went into the kitchen to make him a sandwich but when I came back in, he was fast asleep. He looked so ill and his colour was pale. The fatigue had made him feel exhausted and I was worried about him. I thought now the chemo had ended there would be some relief for him.

The 22nd August was Billy's 58th birthday and all the family arrived at the house for a birthday tea. Billy hadn't been well, and he was trying not to show it. He was tired and in pain and he had planned to sleep when everyone went home. I was in the kitchen when Colin and Paul came in and the family were concerned about Billy. He was pale and I knew something was very wrong. I took his temperature and it was high. I then phoned the Cancer Centre helpline and was told to bring him in. Billy was admitted and had blood tests taken. When the results came back, he needed a blood transfusion and antibiotics. He was annoyed because, just when he thought he was making progress, something would flare up. He was in hospital for a few days and he was feeling low. At times he wanted to be out in the fresh air but his mobility was now affected so I had to get a wheelchair for him and then we went down in the lift and outside in the air for a short time.

He enjoyed this but it wasn't long before he would feel cold. The staff were so good to him and every day he would ask if he could go home yet. He loved it when he could phone me to come and get him, he was always happy to be coming home. Now the chemo was finished, he had to rest and recover. His next appointment would be to have a scan the following week and then to see the consultant to see if the chemo had shrunk the tumours.

The first week in September, the weather was warm, and Billy decided we should go shopping. He had been resting for a few days and now he seemed to have more energy. We went to a shopping centre as I wanted some new candles and then we had a short walk about. We talked of getting a new sofa to match the recliner chair and well, why not do it today? Off we went to a furniture store and got a sofa that was the perfect match. Billy was getting tired so we went home so he could rest. It was a lovely day out and for a short time, we were able to forget about cancer and hospital appointments. It had felt normal, the way it used to be. I didn't realise it then, but that was the last shopping trip he was able to do. I was glad he picked out the new sofa.

On 13th September, Billy saw the consultant and we were told he had responded well to chemo and the tumours had indeed shrunk. However, I felt that Billy was disappointed because he was expecting it to be better news. This is where things became more stressful for me. Chemotherapy had been a lifeline that Billy had been thrown but the consultant had told us that his cancer was terminal, and his treatment would be palliative. He was also in considerable pain, so the consultant made an appointment for him to begin high dose radiotherapy. They also arranged for oxygen to be brought to the house. We had a larger cylinder for the house and a small portable one to take in the car. I was also concerned that he had lost more weight. As each week went by, the picture seemed to change, and we found ourselves dealing with different circumstances. When he didn't feel like eating, the doctor had prescribed vitamin drinks for him to take.

Of course, Billy had to have all the different flavours and depending on his mood, I'd be shouting from the kitchen, 'banana, strawberry or vanilla.' He would tell me I was his beck and call girl! We still managed to laugh.

Billy began radiotherapy and it helped with the pain levels. We had to go to the hospital every morning, but we never had to wait long. There were no side effects and his appetite began to improve. His mood also improved as did his energy levels. We got back down to the boat again and he loved that. For a time, he got a break from feeling so ill and I cherished every minute. He still got tired but after a rest he would feel better and his pain management was better controlled. This was a good time for us both, Billy spent time on the boat with Colin and Julie. He and I also went down to the boat, just for the day, but it was a lovely day. We had lunch at the marina, and we sat on the deck of the boat, just talking. Being at Lough Erne was like a different world for a short time. It was calm and beautiful, and Billy and I were relaxed, just like it used to be. It got cold and I knew it was time to go home. I could see the tiredness in his face and when I helped him to the car, I noticed he was breathless, so I gave him some oxygen. I also carried his toolbox to the car, well, not exactly. I got a wheelbarrow and brought it down to the boat as Billy wanted to bring a few things home. He couldn't have carried stuff himself, so the wheelbarrow came in useful. When we were leaving the marina that day, I had a feeling we wouldn't be back here together again, and I was sad. There were times Billy looked at me, and we didn't speak but we both knew what we were both feeling and what lay ahead. Sometimes a hug was all we needed.

Towards the end of October, Billy began to deteriorate. His appetite wasn't great, and he got tired so easily. We needed to use the oxygen every time he went upstairs and having a shower exhausted him. He never asked to go back down to the boat. He said the weather was getting too cold. I was struggling with my health as I'd had several flare ups with fibromyalgia.

I'd also seen a Consultant about the pain in my spine that was affecting my legs. He told me I needed surgery and he would arrange it but then I had to tell him that it wasn't possible for me to do that now. I had to look after Billy and trying to fit in spinal surgery just wasn't going to work for me. We agreed that he would review me in 6 months, or I could phone his secretary if I needed to.

Throughout the time Billy was ill, my way of coping was to rely on God. My faith and my relationship with him were my solid foundation. When everything around me seemed to be falling apart, I had him to lean on. I would wake up early and go downstairs and make tea and sit in the living room, this was my time to pray, to read my bible and receive the strength I needed for that day. I couldn't have been able to look after Billy without surrendering myself to God each day. At the end of the day when I felt tired, I was thankful for what we had accomplished. Billy still liked to stay up later than me and watch television, while I went to bed to read. But I'd noticed he had begun to come to bed earlier. He was too tired to stay up late. Lying next to Billy, listening to him breathing, I was thankful for another day together and another night of holding one another, until the pain made even that too uncomfortable. I felt so angry at times as I watched the cancer steal a little more of him and I knew he was fighting for his life and he was becoming more exhausted. I used to listen to him breathing while he slept. I had to cherish every moment.

Our daily routine became one of pain management, hoping Billy could eat something or I'd make him smoothies, anything to get sustenance into him. He slept more and was content to be at home. He didn't ask to go out anywhere. We had his computer connected to the television as he could no longer go up and down the stairs to the computer room. Anything to make his life a little more comfortable. The family came often and Billy loved to see them yet as soon as people left, he was asleep.

When I could get out to church on a Sunday morning, I really enjoyed it. It also meant Billy got the house to himself and he would have the computer on and he liked some quiet time on his own. I got a lot of support from people at church and I received strength during worship that would help to carry me through. One morning, towards the end of the service, we sang a song and the words were projected on a screen on the wall. After we had finished, I looked up at the screen and it showed a picture of the planets and galaxies and lots of stars, the graphics were great.

As I was looking at it, in my spirit, I had a picture of Billy and his spirit soaring, leaving everything behind. Then the Holy Spirit spoke to my heart. He said that Billy's spirit would surpass the heavens and that from this day I would look at him through different eyes, I would see him differently and this would be a time of preparation for what lay ahead. In my heart I felt so much love and compassion and I knew the time Billy and I had together was short. However, I felt secure that God was still in control and even in the worst of circumstances, he is still my strength and it is his grace that carries me through.

On Sunday 11th November we had a quiet, relaxing day. Billy watched television or was on the computer and I did a few things around the house and made some dinner. Billy had pain medication as and when he needed it and I remember it was a nice day for us. I went to bed before Billy as I liked to read, and I left him watching a movie. I fell asleep and when I woke up, I was aware that it was late, Billy still hadn't come to bed and it was very quiet. I couldn't hear the television. Suddenly I panicked, I thought something had happened to Billy while I was asleep. I ran downstairs and he was in the living room, the television was off, and he was sitting quietly. I asked him if he was ok and he nodded his head.

I knew he wasn't ok. I picked up a cushion and knelt on the floor in front of him. He became quite emotional and we held hands. He told me he was sorry that he had to leave me soon, we talked about the family and he said I had to move on with my life.

I tried so hard not to cry, but we both did. We said we loved each other, and I knew in my heart that I was losing him, and he was letting me know that he knew it too. We both felt raw and vulnerable, yet it was a conversation that we needed to have. We went to bed and he slept. I lay awake just listening to him breathe and inside my heart was already breaking. I didn't want to face this; I didn't want to be the one that was left behind. I fell asleep with tears running down my face as I turned towards Billy and held him.

On Monday 12 November, Billy had an appointment at the Bridgewater Suite. The clinic was busy that day and we just managed to get two seats. I had the feeling we were in for a long day and I could tell Billy was already feeling exhausted. I got him a coffee and biscuits and whatever way he lifted the cup, it was too hot for him, and he dropped it. I immediately grabbed lots of paper towels and began to clean it up. I told him it didn't matter; I'd get him another one. He was annoyed at himself and that bothered me. He was facing cancer, yet spilling coffee upset him. He settled and I got him a fresh cup. I couldn't help but notice how tired he looked, and I worried that he would be here all day. Eventually we were called in to see the nurse for blood tests and then had to go back outside to the waiting area again. I offered to go and get him a sandwich, but he said he wasn't hungry. Time moved on slowly.

At last we were called to see the consultant. She went over his file and asked him questions. Billy was quite emotional, and he talked freely about his condition and how he had accepted the prognosis. He shared his concerns for me and his family. The Consultant was very understanding and talked about increasing his pain medication as needed. I sat beside Billy and he held my hand. He was told to come back in two weeks, and we left the clinic. Driving home, Billy was so tired, and he complained of being cold. It had been a long emotional day for him, and he was exhausted.

As soon as we got home, I made him comfortable in the recliner chair and gave him his pain medication. He had his blanket over him, and he asked for a sandwich. After he had eaten a little, he slept.

At 8pm the phone rang, and it was the hospital. The blood tests that had been taken that day had shown infection and I was to bring him in. I said he was sleeping, and I'd bring him over in the morning, but the doctor insisted, he had an infection and they wanted him in that night for intravenous antibiotics. I packed a hospital bag and then woke Billy with the news. He wasn't happy. I was told to bring him to ward 3 and Billy had been in that ward a few times and he liked it there, so he was ok about it.

When I think back to that night, I still feel annoyed with myself. I feel I should have insisted on keeping him at home that night, I know he had an infection but the reality was, Billy was dying of lung cancer and one more night at home would have meant so much to both of us.

I took Billy to ward 3 and stayed late until he was settled and on antibiotics. It was dark and cold when I left the cancer centre and as I drove home, I cried. I had this awful feeling that Billy might not be home again. I got home and made tea, then sent Billy a text message and went to bed. I felt exhausted and I slept for a few hours but when I woke up, I had to get to the hospital. I needed to see Billy. There was an urgency to get to the hospital. When I arrived, he was sitting up in bed and he asked me to take him outside for some fresh air. Now he was on an antibiotic intravenous drip and I also needed a wheelchair. He had his dressing gown on and a blanket over him too. We laughed as we got in the lift as he held onto the drip stand as it was on wheels. We stayed outside a short time, until Billy got cold again.

Billy was kept on antibiotics up until the 17th November, but his condition had begun to deteriorate. The infection wasn't responding to treatment, even when they changed it to a stronger antibiotic. He was sleepy a lot of the time and family came and went for visits but while he was aware of them, he was too ill to talk. The consultant came to see me, and we talked privately. She told me that Billy was no longer responding to treatment and the time had come to consider what is called, pathway for the dying.

She thought that Billy didn't have long left to live and this should be more about keeping him comfortable and pain free. She also suggested I begin to stay at night with him. I agreed with her and steps were put in place.

Billy had been in a small ward with three other patients but now we were moved to a private room. While they got him settled some of our family arrived and I told them what was happening.

Julie and Colin went to my house to get some clothes and toiletries I might need. I wasn't leaving Billy. The staff offered to put another bed in the room for me, but I said no. I wanted to be beside him so they brought me in a recliner chair and I was able to sit beside his bed and at night I could sleep for a while. Over the next few days, Billy's antibiotics were stopped, and he was given pain relief. A syringe driver was put in place for his pain medication and everything was done to make him as comfortable as possible. The family all knew what was happening and visitors began to arrive. Billy was conscious and able to hold a conversation for some of the time, but he got tired. His mum and sister came in and I felt sad for his mother, she had had more than her share of family heartache, having lost her husband and two daughters and now, Billy, her eldest son was dying. In the coming days, all our family and his made regular visits and our children were there every day. Colin came and stayed with his dad while I'd go for a walk for ten minutes to clear my head. Carol came, and she brought me a little crystal teddy bear and it said, thinking of you on it. Carol was Billy's first wife and she and I always got along, she was and still is a lovely thoughtful person. I still have that little teddy bear. My family came to visit too and at one point the staff had to get extra chairs to fit into the room. During the day, Julie, Colin and Paul and Roisin called in, as Billy could have visits anytime. Billy was always aware of what was going on, but he got tired easily.

My time with Billy was when everyone went home. The staff would come in to settle Billy for the night and someone would bring me a cup of tea. I left only the dimmer lights on and the room was quiet and cosy. I would sit on the chair beside Billy and talk to him until he was tired enough for sleep. Billy and I had often talked about his relationship with God and now when we talked, I prayed with him. He was at peace about what was happening to him and had come to a place of acceptance about his life ending. I was relieved to see him at peace.

Sometimes during the night, he would wake, and it sounded like he was choking. The first time this happened I pushed the bell and a nurse came in and raised up the bed until he settled. He could take sips of water through a straw. I watched her and I thought that I'd know what to do. However, it happened the next day when I was alone with him and he had been in a sleep when he suddenly began to choke. My instinct was to raise the bed with the remote control but in my panic, I put Billy down instead of up. He was nearly upside down and I was frightened. Panicking, I muttered my apologies and quickly adjusted the bed upwards as I pushed the bell for help. The staff explained to me that there was no need to panic, just raise the bed and ring the bell. When the crisis was over, I was shattered! Later when I thought of Billy nearly being upside down, I began to laugh as I apologised to Billy and I thought, this could only happen to me!

Billy began to deteriorate daily, and he slept more. He could no longer eat, and he was on intravenous fluids. I would use little swab sticks dipped in ice water to keep his lips and mouth moist. Family came every day and as our room had an en-suite, I was able to have a shower while someone sat with Billy. I was getting used to staying in the hospital and I didn't allow myself to think about how long we would have left. I didn't take each day as it came but I took each hour of each day. On Wednesday 21st November, we had the usual day of Billy being cared for and made comfortable by the staff. They were so good to him and to me and my family.

Early in the morning a lovely woman would knock the door and come in and she would bring me tea and toast. A male nurse would look in on Billy and come and give him a wash and shave and he talked to him, even though Billy wasn't always conscious. That day Billy sat up in the bed and I had my back to him, I was talking to my daughter and I turned as he reached out his hand. I was at his side in seconds as he put his head back and closed his eyes. We had just seen each other for the last time. Billy lost consciousness that day. Visitors came and went but while he may have been aware of them, he could no longer respond. That night, when it was just him and me, I settled in the chair beside him. I was chatting to him because I believed he could still hear.

He settled into sleep but in a short time he was choking and thankfully I stayed calm. A nurse came in and waited until he settled again, and I sat beside him, but he groaned loudly in his sleep and I knew he was suffering. I prayed over him and for a while he was quiet, and the choking started again. This went on unto the early hours of the morning until he finally settled into sleep. This was the worst night we had in his battle with pain.

Thursday the 22nd November and Billy remained unconscious. He was in a peaceful sleep but then he was exhausted. It was a quiet day with a few visitors and Billy remained peaceful. There had been no more choking. That night when everyone had left, I felt exhausted. I prayed for a peaceful night. The staff settled Billy and checked his medication, I had a cup of tea and chatted to Billy for a few minutes. Switching off the light, I fell asleep holding Billy's hand. Early the next morning I woke around 5:30am. I realised that Billy and I had slept all night without waking. I went to the window and pulled up the blind and the sky outside was amazing. The colours of amber, pinks and blues were like God had just painted me a beautiful picture. I smiled and said thank you and, in my spirit, I heard him say that Billy was going home today. I was thankful we had had a peaceful night together.

Just then a nurse came in and said that she had checked on us a few times during the night, but we were both sound asleep. Again, I said thank you to God. The morning routine began, and I was calm, and Billy was in a peaceful sleep. I sat beside him, and I'd been reading when I noticed his breathing getting slower. I talked to him and whispered in his ear that I loved him. At 9:10am Billy took one last breath and then silence. I held him and as I did, I could see in my spirit a portal opening in the heavens and Billy's spirit left his body quickly. It was over. I held him for a few minutes and then rang the bell. A nurse came in and I told her that Billy had gone but I needed time on my own to let him go. She told me to take my time and ring for her when I felt ready. I held Billy until I knew it was time for me to say goodbye.

His suffering was over, and he was at peace and I was thankful to God for that peace. His life on earth was over and I was no longer his wife but a widow. I rang for the nurse and then the doctor came and confirmed his death. It was Friday 23rd November 2007.

I began to ring the family and tell them the news and of course they quickly got to the hospital. They had to say their own goodbyes. The staff attended to Billy with so much respect. They were amazing. As a family we began to pack Billy belongings to bring home and all the stuff that I had. Billy was at peace and I stroked his face and kissed him. Finally, we had to say goodbye and it was so hard for all of us. I knew once we left that room, nothing would ever be the same again. Billy was dead and our time at the cancer centre had ended. We left the room and the doctor gave us the death certificate.

Leaving the ward and going down in the lift to the ground floor I felt such a separation in my heart. As we walked towards the doors leading to outside, I stopped. I couldn't do it. I turned to go back to the lift. I didn't want to leave Billy. I had been with him 24/7 and now I was going home without him and I wasn't coming back. It was too much for me. I just wanted to go and stay with him. My family was amazing, they got me outside in the fresh air and I began to take deep breaths. My car was still in the car park and I knew once I got to the car, I would be alright.

We arranged to meet back at my house. Julie was going to register the death and then we were going to go to the funeral home as a family to make the arrangements. I got into my car and put the window down and just breathed in the fresh air. I began to drive, but driving away from the cancer centre, I was heartbroken. Billy wouldn't be coming home with me anymore; it was over, and I didn't know how I was getting through this. I cried as I drove home. I hadn't been home since I'd been staying with Billy and as I walked into our house, it felt strange that Billy wouldn't be here again.

I went upstairs to our bedroom and sat on the bed and cried. I was relieved that Billy was no longer suffering and for him it was over, and he was in heaven. I was fifty-three and I remember thinking that I was too young to be a widow! Billy was fifty-eight. I was sad that we wouldn't get to do all the things we had planned to do. In that moment before the family arrived, I prayed for the strength to get through the day. Part of me felt numb inside, as if this weren't really happening yet I knew it was real. Shock is a wonderful thing at times like this. I felt that God had given me a big cushion to fall on and he would carry me through. I remembered the night that I had broken a bone in my hand and my wedding ring had to be cut off, I'd be so upset as I'd experienced such a feeling of loss. Now I knew I was being prepared for losing Billy. Eleven months had gone by since that night and now his life was over. He had bought me new rings, but I still have the one that was cut.

Colin, Julie and Paul took me down to the funeral home and arrangements were made for the funeral. Billy's body would be brought to the funeral home on Saturday and the funeral would be on Monday 26th November. That date was also Julie's birthday, she wanted to share the day with him. We requested family flowers only as we thought a donation to the Cancer Centre would be more appropriate. I'll never forget the care shown to Billy while he was there, and the staff were amazing with the family.

I went to see Billy in the funeral home, and I was surprised at how young he looked. His suffering now over and he was at peace. I was missing him already and I couldn't think any further than the day I was living in. Beyond that was just too much.

The day of the funeral was a sort of blur for me. I was aware of the many people who came for the service in the funeral church. I went in to see Billy one last time and I remember feeling so empty inside. The coffin was brought into the church with a spray of white roses and lilies on the top and a captain's cap personalised with Billy's name that Colin had gotten for his dad when he bought the boat.

Julie had written the eulogy and I want to include it here.

'A number of different reasons have brought us together here today. Many of us are family. Some of us are friends and acquaintances. Some of you weren't lucky enough to meet William Murray Holmes, but are here to show your support to the rest of us who mourn him now.

Those of us who had him in our lives all knew him by different names. He was Murray. Billy. Sticky. To me, he was Dad. Or sometimes daddy if I was after something! Mum sometimes called him different names again, but that's another story...

For myself and my younger brother Paul, he wasn't always our Dad. He met our mum when I was 12 and Paul was 10.

For 2 young kids, it was great to have someone around who could take us for long drives, buy us endless supplies of junk food, teach us how to fish and let us watch horror videos. The best part though, was that we inherited a big brother – although Colin is actually shorter than both of us now! – and, for me, it was great that he lived with his mum because I got to have the benefits of having a big brother but still be the eldest at home.

When Mum and Dad got married, we didn't just have a man about the house. Dad was really good with animals, so we also adopted his dog.

He trained her as a gun dog, and he went hunting a lot. I will always remember the first time he got me to eat chicken stew and didn't tell me till afterwards that it was actually rabbit.

Then came the budgie. Anyone here who was ever in our house at the time will remember Joey. And not fondly, as he used to lurk on top of the light and dive-bomb any visitors just as they got comfortable. Dad taught him to talk. And drink beer. It was a cute party trick until one night, Joey fell into Dad's pint glass of beer and Dad had to fish him out by the tail. The poor wee budgie staggered across the floor saying, 'poor poor wee Joey' repeatedly while Dad laughed at him.

Dad loved gadgets and quirky things that no one else would seriously buy. He had shelves full of those executive desk toys, magnetic things that made balls look like they were floating in mid-air and weird wee lights. He always had to know how everything worked. He liked to take things apart just to see if he could put them back together again.

Dad's love of gadgets extended to gadgets of a much bigger type. When he was younger, he used to race motorbikes. If he didn't win, he told me he would take the bike apart and put it back together again. With extras. Mum was relieved when he bought a decent BMW motorbike which didn't need to be taken apart and went when he got on it. That meant she wasn't afraid to get on it either. They christened the bike Betsy, and they used to take Betsy up the north coast to White Park Bay every summer.

Dad was always tinkering at something. In recent years, his fascination moved from bikes to boats. This year he fulfilled a very long ambition to own his own cabin cruiser. He said he 'rescued 'her from an auction. He named her, 'New Beginnings'. He said these were new beginnings for the boat, new beginnings politically in Northern Ireland with the return of a devolved government.

And new beginnings for our family, as we would have the boat to create many happy holidays and good memories for a long time to come.

That was in April. Sadly. Dad found out a few weeks later that he had lung cancer and had only months to live. That didn't stop him tinkering at the boat though. In fact, it made him relieved that he had gotten the boat at last and he was even more determined that his family would enjoy the boat for years to come. That was a lovely notion. It wasn't so lovely when he was trying to teach Colin and I to moor the boat and it ended up with a nice dent in the front. Dad really wanted to take New Beginnings down the Shannon before he died. He never got to do that. But we will do it next summer in his honour.

I've said a lot of nice things about Dad and shared a lot of fond memories. I know he is listening, and he's waiting for the catch... There isn't one. Well not really... Dad was no angel. And he would be the first to say it. We had a lot of ups and downs as a family. Bad times as well as good. Distance as well as closeness. Like many families do.

For me though, I think a person can be judged by two things, 1- did people love you in life? 2 – will people miss you in death?

1 – Was my Dad loved in life? Without a doubt. My Dad was loved by his family and friends and respected by people who hardly even knew him. He had a very gentle, warm way about him. He would have done a favour for anyone. People always spoke fondly of him.

And when it came near the end, the hospital staff at the cancer centre had to bring out more chairs to accommodate the number of visitors wanting to see him before he died.

2 – Will my Dad be missed in death? Look around this room. There is your answer.

I thank God that he chose me to be my Dad's daughter. I was blessed to have him. He gave me anything I ever asked for. He did everything for me that he physically could. All three of us have given Dad plenty of cause for concern over the years. But he never judged. Never got impatient. He just accepted us. No questions.

It's been a long time since I was at church, but today I'm reminded of a particular passage from the bible that I would like to share with you now. It reminds me of my Dad. Here it is:

'Love is patient. Love is kind. It does not envy, it does not boast, it is not proud. It is not rude, it is not self-seeking, it is not easily angered, it keeps no record of wrongs. Love does not delight in evil but rejoices in the truth. It always protects, always trusts, always hopes, always perseveres. Love never dies.'

My Dad's legacy is that he taught me how to love unconditionally, and as a parent now myself I think that is the single most important lesson he could ever have taught me. That will never die. He will live on through me, through his sons and in his grandsons.

Now and always.

After the service the funeral proceeded to Carmoney cemetery and there was another short service at the grave. We then walked away, and I was thinking, is this it?

I had booked a hotel for a buffet afterwards for family and friends and by the time it was over, it was late afternoon. I remember feeling so tired and drained. Julie wanted me to go home with her, but I just wanted to go home and be on my own. I felt exhausted. When I got home, I was aware of the silence when I shut the front door. I'd no energy left to cry, and I felt shut down inside. I went to bed and slept. When I woke up it was early morning and I was still so tired. I was suddenly aware of not having to go to the Cancer Centre every day because Billy was no longer there. I felt lost and didn't know what to do with myself. In every room in the house there was something that belonged to him and it still felt like he should be coming home. I was weary mentally and emotionally and was having a flare up of pain with fibromyalgia. I had a few days rest and then decided to tackle some jobs in the house. There were lots of Billy's medications that had to be returned to the chemist and slowly I began to sort through stuff.

In one way I felt better for doing it, yet it was hard to accept that Billy was gone, and I was on my own. Since his death I had felt like God had given me a big cushion to fall on and the emotional shock was a safe place for me to be. Eventually the cushion would be taken away because God is a God of reality and I would have to face the fact that

Billy was dead. It happened when I wasn't really expecting it. I went out to get some shopping and I nearly put items in the shopping trolley that Billy liked and then I thought, no, I don't buy that anymore. I got home and unpacked the car and brought the shopping into the hall. As I closed the front door there was an echo, then silence and I thought, I'm never going to hear Billy's key in the door anymore. Suddenly something broke inside me and I felt in a panic. Going into the kitchen to put the kettle on, I began to cry and slide down onto the floor and cried for such a long time. I felt drained and cold after a while and I wondered why I hadn't just gone into the living room and sat in a chair!

I went to bed early that night and I felt something had been torn from my heart. Emotionally I was raw and fragile. Over the next few days, I was exhausted and didn't know how I was going to cope with life. I kept forgetting he wasn't here, and I'd go to put his coffee mug out when I boiled the kettle. I still thought of making the dinner for both of us and wondered what he would like.

I knew the whole time he was ill that one day this would happen, and I'd be on my own but the reality of that is so painful. I had so much to learn about being a widow. My mind had been so used to thinking about 'us' and now it was 'me'. I could no longer think about what we were having for dinner, instead it was what do I make for myself? Baked potatoes in the microwave became a favourite.

It felt lonely at times and when I went to bed, I still liked to read but it took ages to get to sleep. I went from being sad to feeling angry that he was gone. We had made so many plans for the future, but we didn't have a future now and I felt empty. I prayed a lot and read my bible because I knew I needed my relationship with the Lord to bring me through this grief.

One morning I was awake very early, and it was quiet and peaceful. I was half asleep, yet my spirit was very alert. In my spirit I saw Billy walk into the bedroom and he looked lovely. He was wearing his suit and I could smell his body spray. We looked at each other but no words were exchanged, yet we communicated with our thoughts. We each knew what the other one was thinking. He was letting me know he was alright, and I'd be alright, and he smiled at me. He reached out his hand and I held it and his skin was soft and warm. Then I knew he had to go, and I didn't want him to go, I wanted just a few more moments. He let go of my hand and walked toward the door. He stopped and looked back, and I smiled at him. I knew this was the final goodbye and I wouldn't see him again until I go to heaven. Suddenly he was gone, and I was wide awake, and I looked at my hand and it was still closed over like it had been when I had held Billy's hand.

I began to cry yet I was thankful to God that he had allowed me to experience one last goodbye and to experience the peace that was now Billy's. I loved him and I missed him and right at that moment I'd have gone with him if I could. I realised that our last goodbye was closure on this life and now I would have to learn to live again without him.

One of the things I had to face was the amount of administration and form filling that had to be done when someone dies. I had to deal with the finances, there was still a mortgage on the house and then there was the life insurance company. I lost count of the number of death certificates Julie got for me because everybody wanted one! At a time when I really didn't want to do this, it was the thing that helped me. It gave me something to focus on.

Billy died four weeks before Christmas and it felt so different without him. He used to do all the cooking and he loved Christmas shopping. I found myself keeping things as easy and simple as possible. My food shop was a lot smaller that year! Every year Billy and I used to take Christmas wreaths up to the cemetery for family graves. I used to order them especially for my parent's grave, Billy's sister and his dad. I placed the order as usual and then realised I needed one more for Billy's grave. The afternoon I went up to Carmoney cemetery was a dull cold day. I placed the wreaths on the family graves and made my way to Billy's grave. Where he was buried was a new plot and there was no proper pathway, just boards to walk on and it was really mucky. His was a new grave with just a marker as I wouldn't be able to get the headstone for a few months. I placed the wreath on the grave and I began to cry, and I couldn't stop. I was kneeling in the soil and then it got dark and the heavy rain started. I was heartbroken. I knew I had to move, well, as I tried to stand up, my foot got stuck and when I tried to pull it out of the soil the other one got stuck. My boots kept sinking further every time I tried to pull one out. I realised I was in trouble and there was no one about. I had to crawl on my hand and knees to the wooden boards so that I could stand up and by this time I was soaking wet with the rain and I was covered in muck. I got back to my car and when I looked in the mirror, my mascara was down my face and my eyes were black. I was so upset, and I was relieved to drive away. As I drove I thought about my feet sinking in the soil, and how worried I was that I wouldn't get out of it, I suddenly began to laugh, I'm sure Billy would have been laughing too.

I called into the garden centre on my way home and it was all lit up with Christmas lights. I felt so empty inside and I decided I wasn't going to bother with a tree that year. Then I saw a lovely fibre optic tree and I bought it, brought it home and plugged it in and that was it, Merry Christmas.

I found Christmas Eve difficult because Billy and I used to open one present before bed, have a glass of wine and it was lovely. I found it strange being without him that night. The next day I was going to see my family for dinner, and I got through the day alright. Driving home, I felt so tired. I seem to be experiencing this weariness a lot. I rested over the next few days and spent some time reading. I felt grief had broken my heart and only God could help me to heal. That first Christmas without Billy was so hard but resting and taking the time to begin to heal helped.

New Years came and went, and my days seem to drift past. I'd been in pain with my spine and usually when I had a flare up of pain, I would rest in bed and Billy would bring me cups of tea and a sandwich.

That didn't happen anymore, and I missed him.

I thought back to the previous year when we had enjoyed Christmas with family and being together. It was a lovely holiday time and we didn't realise then that it would be Billy's last Christmas. When Billy died, I felt such an incredible loss. Every activity reminded me of him. Going to the supermarket and hearing a song being played that we both liked reduced me to tears.

Learning to shop just for myself was different, admittedly it was cheaper! At nighttime before I went to bed, I had to check the doors were locked and everything switched off, that had been Billy's job. I even had to learn to put the wheelie bin out! To this day I hate putting the bin out. Something in me still says, 'that's Billy's job.'

Life is such a learning curve and there is so much I am thankful for. Learning to drive the year before Billy got ill, I was able to drive him to the hospital for his appointments. Now he is gone I had the car which helped me remain independent especially with my own health problems. At times when I pray, it's like I take a step back from the life that I see and when I look in my spirit, I can see how God prepares the way. There is nothing that is out of his control. He is always there and whatever happens in life is not a surprise to him. My security rests in him because he will always bring me through whatever circumstances I find myself in.

When Billy died, I remembered the morning I was in church and God had shown me that Billy's spirit would surpass the heavens. I wrote a little verse for the newspaper obituary.

Your journey has been painful, I watched you suffer to the end. In my life you were my love, my soulmate and my friend. But there's a greater One who calls you and it is God's time for you to leave, He whispered, you are weary, take my hand and come to Me.

I love you and I'll miss you; you'll always be a part of me, but one day we'll be together for all eternity. Now you are safe with Jesus and from sickness you are free. As your spirit surpasses the heavens, you are who you were meant to be.

Fly free my love and soar.

Chapter 15

After my husband died, I found I struggled with accepting little details in life that I didn't have to deal with when he was here. I struggled with the word, 'widow.' The first time I came up against it, I was filling in a form and I automatically went to tick, married in the little box and then I suddenly remembered that I was no longer a married person but a widow. I didn't like it. It felt as though a part of me was now missing and the death of my husband changed my status. I was fifty-three and I never thought this would happen to me. Being in a second marriage, I thought we would be together until old age. Death is more acceptable if it happens very late in life, it's an end of life. I certainly didn't expect to be filling in forms and ticking the widow box in my fifties!

I felt incredibly lonely and the path ahead of me seemed dark. I wasn't sure how I would cope with life now. My one security was being a relationship with God. I had that sense of belonging that I needed. One of the hardest things I found was how life still goes on, even though I felt my world was standing still. When Billy was ill and especially the times when he was in hospital, I seemed to cope because he was still here, and I was able to look after him.

The family came more often, and I was always thinking of the next stage of his treatment. Now it was January 2008 and life for my family had to go on. They had jobs and children and their own grief. I had that feeling of my world being turned upside down and now it was still, and I didn't know how to move on.

I had to go into town one morning. I was still sorting out life insurance and I'd a meeting at the probate office. I got there and then did some shopping before going home. I used to forget Billy was no longer here and then when I opened the front door the silence would echo. I didn't cry very often but that day I remember feeling overwhelmed with everything. I never realised how much form filling and paperwork was involved when someone died. It was the days of being overwhelmed and fatigued that I would burst into tears and cry until I was too tired to cry anymore. Picking up a photograph of him and I down at the boat I cried as though my heart was breaking. We had planned so many trips on New Beginnings and there had been so much to look forward to. Now it was never going to happen, and I'd go from feeling sad to feeling angry. Emotionally I was exhausted. I spend more time with the Lord and read my bible more. I talked to him about everything and I wrote in my journal most days. I was in constant pain coming from my spine and the fibromyalgia had flared badly. I made an appointment with the doctor and she referred me back to the consultant.

It was wintertime and I wasn't out much. The cold intensified the pain, so I stayed home more in the heat. I got an appointment with the consultant on 1st March, and when I went to see him, I was told I would need an operation to repair a damaged disc at the bottom of my spine. I expected there would be a waiting list and I was surprised when a letter came a few weeks later with a date for my operation. It was in April and I was being sent to Blackpool. I immediately panicked because Billy wasn't here to go with me. I really got in a state about it. I was so annoyed that Billy had died, and I had now to do life on my own. My mood was very low for days. I just didn't want to face life anymore.

Being a widow was too hard. I wondered if it would have been any easier if I'd had a job to go back to after Billy died. Yet, I think it would have been hard, regardless of my circumstances. I'd lost my husband and I missed him. I found some days harder than others but there was no pattern to my life. I literally took each day as it arrived. One day when I was spending time in prayer, the Holy Spirit showed me a picture of a wooden doll. It was one of those dolls that separated and there was a doll within a doll, each one getting smaller until there was just one tiny one left. Each doll seemed to represent a period of time in my life, times when I made choices that seemed the right thing to do at that particular time. Time that was for my marriage, my family and church and I made decisions that I knew were expected of me. Deep inside I had my dreams and desires, but it wasn't the right time for them, everything else had to come first. I saw me hold the last doll in my hand and it was the smallest and I felt that this was me right now. I felt so small and yet in my spirit I saw that the doll also represented my dreams that I had carried for many years. A glimmer of hope ignited inside me and I believed that although I was grieving, I would eventually move on from this place and my heart would heal. I believed there would be a new beginning for me.

My sister Ruth decided to come with me to Blackpool. My family had full time jobs and young children of their own so it would have been more difficult for them to have to arrange things. I would have preferred to be going to a hospital in Belfast, but Blackpool had a date sooner, so it was set.

On Sunday 13th April, Ruth and I went to the airport to fly to Blackpool. It was a lovely day and I was relaxed and ready for the journey. When we arrived in Blackpool, we got a taxi to the Hilton hotel, where we were booked in. Our room was lovely, and we had dinner that night in the restaurant. The next morning, the 14th, we left early for the hospital. I was booked in and shown to my room which I shared with another lady who was also having spinal surgery. After I saw the doctor, I was taken to theatre at 2.30pm and the best bit for me is when they gave me the anaesthetic.

I loved that feeling of my body relaxing and drifting off to sleep. I know some people are afraid of that, but I've had fibromyalgia for a number of years and at times my muscles go into spasm. I had been on several drugs for this condition so when I got the anaesthetic and my muscles relaxed, it felt amazing, and then I went to sleep.

When I woke up later that day, I was aware of having pain down my legs. My spine was painful but that was post-op pain. I was given pain relief although I felt very cold. I was on a drip for fluids and they were concerned about my blood pressure as it was very low. The nurse was in and out the room several times and I just remember feeling so tired.

My sister Ruth was beside my bed and I was puzzled when I looked at her because she looked different. I thought maybe I was just a bit confused, but I said to her that she looked different and I was right. She told me that while I was in the theatre she went for a walk into town and went into a hair salon and had her hair done! She did buy me a postcard of Blackpool with a butterfly on the front. I've always liked butterflies and I still have that card. I was kept in the hospital until Wednesday and then I was discharged, and we went back to the hotel. I had little energy and I was in pain. We had dinner and then began to pack for the return journey home the next day.

My spine was covered in a large dressing as I had stitches in, and Ruth was left with the luggage the next morning.

We got a taxi to the airport and Ruth was struggling with the luggage, I laughed as she tried to keep hold of it all. A porter saw us and came over and offered to help. He took the cases and got a wheelchair for me. Ruth thought she should have been the one pushed in the chair. When we got to board the plane, I was taken up a ramp in the chair that brought me up to the door of the plane. Ruth went on in and waved at me from the window. I felt like I was on a builder's ramp getting hoisted up onto the plane. My pride got slightly dented!

Arriving in Belfast, Ruth's husband Fred was waiting for us. Soon I was on my way home and I was so glad to see my house. We had dinner and then they went home, and I settled in the recliner chair and it felt so good to be back. I slept well that night although Billy was my first thought when I woke up. I missed him and I'd have loved him to have been here with me.

The next day a nurse called to the house to change the dressing on my back. This continued for a week and then the stitches came out. I was still sore, but I put that down to post-op pain. I hoped that within a few weeks it would all settle, and I'd be feeling better. I found it difficult being at home and coping with my recovery without Billy. Everything I tried to do required more effort as I was so tired. I was told that fatigue after an operation was normal and I had to rest in order to recover. The initial few weeks after I came home were the hardest as I was at home and I wasn't allowed to drive, so I was stuck in the house with the exception of a walk out the back of the house.

We had the garden taken away and it was paved in, so I was able to sit out in the sun for a while. I was still experiencing pain in my lower spine and had to take medication. My best times were reading my bible or writing in my journal and just spending time with the Lord. I find that sitting still in his presence can be so calming and restful.

In July I was able to arrange for the headstone to go on Billy's grave. Julie came with me to choose one and I decided on a grey marble one with gold writing. A lovely woman helped us decide on the writing and then I suggested a picture of Billy's boat would be nice. I was able to give her a photograph of New Beginnings and it was sketched in gold onto the marble stone. Since headstones are quite expensive and when my name goes on it, I'm not going to be here to see it. I suggested putting something on for me. The woman reminded me that I'm not dead yet so what was I thinking? Like I said, headstones are expensive, and I thought I should have something. As I like to write, it was decided that a gold open book would be put in the corner opposite the boat. I was happy with that.

When the headstone went on the grave and we went up to see it, I was really pleased with it and sure enough, in one corner was Billy's boat and in the opposite is my book. I was happy!

As the weeks went on, I expected to see an improvement in my health. The pain in my spine was dragging me down and the fibromyalgia had flared badly. I struggled with pain and fatigue and it was at those times that I missed Billy so much. It was an effort for me to look after myself and cooking was usually something out of the freezer and into the microwave. I also felt on an emotional roller coaster and my mood was quite low. I went to see the doctor and she put me on antidepressants and referred me back to Musgrave Park Hospital regarding my spine. I thought the operation I had would have taken care of the pain I was in but now it was there all the time. I knew I'd be back on the waiting list and it would take months but at least we had a plan.

The summer days I would go for a drive and try to keep my mind occupied. I missed Billy because summer was his favourite time to be out on the boat and to go fishing. I longed for those days out on Lough Erne with the breeze blowing and the rays of sunshine on my face.

Some memories are so precious and our times at Carrybridge were so special. We loved the marina at the moorings and going for dinner at the restaurant. At night we would sit on the deck of the boat and it was so beautiful and peaceful, those were the times I wanted to last forever. Yet 2007 had been our last year making memories at Lough Erne.

As the summer gave way to autumn, I became more accepting of my circumstances. Autumn is one of my favourite times of the year. I love to go for a walk and watch the leaves of the trees change colour as they begin to blow from the branches. The path is covered in brown and gold leaves and it reminds me that this is a time for change. By October I had a sense of change deep within me and I was aware of an emptiness that only God could fill.

The stillness in my spirit that told me to wait quietly on him.

Micah 7:7

'As for me, I look to the Lord for help. I wait confidently for God to save me, and my God will certainly hear.' (NLT)

As a woman who was still adapting to being a widow, I realised that I needed to depend on God more and more. My mind was constantly thinking back to the year before when

Billy was so ill, and he battled so hard with cancer. Now I grieved for him. When I felt this way, I would go and have a bath, the scented candles would be lit, and I'd have a nice bath oil in the water. I loved the warmth of the water and the stillness in the atmosphere. This was a relaxing time but also a time when I would pour my heart out to God and be in tears. After a while, when I was beginning to wrinkle, it was time to take a deep breath and know that I would be okay. Everyone has different coping mechanisms, but having a lovely bath was one of mine and it helped. I was discovering that whatever helped me through the grief was a good thing.

I was learning more about grace and how each day with God was a new day drawing on his grace. I was finding myself, my real self in him. I had experienced two marriages, had two amazing children, and came through the single parent years in between the marriages and I thought that Billy and I would be together to old age. I never thought I would be a widow at fifty-three. To find the real self in God I had to put all of this to one side in order to go deeper with Him.

Accepting being widowed was a totally different life to the one I had imagined. I felt so lonely and I knew that only God could meet my needs. I was getting to know Him as a husband and every morning his word revealed more of Him to me. This is the time of falling in love with the Lord all over again. Drawing close to him because I was grieving, I was lonely, and I needed Him more. One of my readings from the Message bible encouraged me.

Isaiah 62:2-5

'...*You'll get a brand new name, straight from the mouth of God, You'll be a stunning crown in the palm of God's hand, a jewelled gold cup held high in the hand of your God. No*

152

more will anyone call you Rejected, and your country will no more be Ruined. You'll be called Hephzibah (My Delight), and your land Beulah (Married) Because God delights in you and your land will be like a wedding celebration. For as a young man marries his virgin bride, so your builder marries you, and as a bridegroom is happy in his bride so your God is happy with you.'

It's in these alone times with God that I was strengthened and during my day, when I had moments of missing Billy, or just remembering, I would draw on something the Lord had given me.

2 Corinthians 12:9 (Message)

'My grace is enough, it's all you need. My strength comes into its own in your weakness.'

I knew the meaning and the depth of those words as the first anniversary of Billy's death approached. The worst time was the two weeks leading up to the date he died. In my mind I relived those days and nights that we spent in the Cancer Centre the year before. I went up to the grave on the 23rd November and it was hard to believe a whole year had passed. I still felt broken and I wondered if I'd ever be whole again. Maybe this pain would always be in my heart, but it would get easier to bear. Kneeling at the grave, placing flowers at the headstone and my emotions giving way to tears, I experienced what God had said, 'My grace is enough, it's all you need.'

Chapter 16

In 2009 I was still struggling with pain in my lower spine. I had another MRI scan at Musgrave Park Hospital, and I didn't have long to wait for the results. Talking with the consultant, I was told I needed to have another spinal operation. I had a trapped nerve and the disc that they had tried to repair at the first operation, needed to come out. That wasn't the news I had wanted to hear but, I understood why I was in so much pain. A few weeks after the consultation, I got an appointment for my pre-op assessment at Musgrave. I was relieved things were moving quicker this time. It was two months later I got a date for the operation and this time it was being done in Belfast. I was so glad I didn't have to travel again. Paul and Roisin took me over to the hospital, I was admitted to the Ulster Independent and I had my own room. They stayed until I was settled. It is a lovely place and the staff were amazing. The first day when I was admitted I had all the checks done and I had a chat with the surgeon. At 7:30 the next morning I was on my way to the theatre. I was nervous but I had a lovely nurse with me called Julie and I told her I'd a daughter called Julie. She stayed with me until I'd been given the anaesthetic and I went to sleep.

I awoke later that day and I was aware of the pain in my spine. The doctor came in and told me the operation went well and then I was given an injection and went to sleep. I knew I was in a deep sleep, yet I could sense the pain and I just wanted it to stop.

My blood pressure was very low and all that night I felt ill. It was like getting pulled down into a big hole of pain. I was aware of nurses checking in with me during the night and eventually I slept through the pain. The next morning a lovely nurse came in and helped to bathe and dress me and I felt so cared for. I had a much better day and felt rested. I was still receiving pain injections when I needed them, but I knew I was in recovery now. I enjoyed the food; my room had a television and I was glad the operation was behind me now. After a few days I was on my way back home again.

I was glad to get home as I missed my own bed. A nurse came out every morning and dressed the wound until it was time for the staples to come out. I felt exhausted and just wanted to rest. Eventually I began to feel better and although I had flare ups with the fibromyalgia, I was managing any pain with medication. I had imagined that over time my health would improve, but two months after the surgery I began to have the lower back pain again. It didn't go down my leg because the nerve that was trapped had been sorted but the pain across my lower back was severe. I was totally baffled. I had undergone two spinal operations in the space of fifteen months, and I didn't expect to still be in pain. I saw my doctor who referred me back to Musgrave Park Hospital. I got an appointment at the day hospital and the morning of my appointment it had snowed heavy during the night. I booked a taxi as my family couldn't get to me to go with me. At the hospital, I was put into a gown and taken to theatre. I had several spinal injections which were painful, but I hoped these would work and the pain would settle. I was told if the pain persisted, I would have to consider a third operation, but it would mean having a spinal infusion, which I didn't want to have. I went home and went to bed and rested and for two weeks I felt better and then gradually the pain came back. I couldn't face another operation, so I felt I was back to square one.

I now use pain management as a way of controlling the level of pain and I've had a lot of physio over the years. Spinal pain affects my lower spine and fibromyalgia affects my whole body. At times, my spine goes into spasm and it's very painful and the spasms aren't limited to my spine. I get them over my body, and it feels like every muscle is paralysed with spasm. Rest and medication help and light exercise, but each day presents new challenges. Fatigue is another symptom that drains me of energy. I have days when I'm able to have a shower and within a short time I am so fatigued I can fall asleep on the chair in the living room. I'm very good at hiding the pain. If I can put on a little make up and smile, then no one would know if I had been awake all night because of the fibromyalgia. Pain is invisible and so is fatigue. Sometimes someone will tell me they think I look very tired but other than that, I can hide it well. I suppose I do this because I don't want to be drawing attention to illness. Also, I find that people would soon get fed up hearing about it.

I have been blessed with a good sense of humour and I can laugh at things, no one else would find funny. I find it easier to try and stay positive as opposed to negative when it comes to health. When I do get days when the pain just feels too much to cope with, then I spend time with the Lord and read my bible or write in my journal. It helps to write down scriptures that refer to healing. In the painful times I have known God's grace carrying me through and his word also brings me above the pain level. I've had to learn to trust in him during the painful days and especially when my energy is low. Living on my own has a lot of advantages, as I do housework when I can, and I don't have to have the same structure every day. It also means I can rest when I need to.

I have learnt to lean into God's grace and rest when I'm going through a flare up of fibromyalgia. Everyone has different coping mechanisms and I have learnt what is best for me. Being quiet and avoiding noise also helps. I remember being in a supermarket and I needed to get home. The pain and fatigue were difficult to handle but the worst thing was the music being played. It was like it was amplified in my brain.

Fibromyalgia has many symptoms but the ones I struggle with are pain, fatigue, noise, anxiety and the worst one can be depression. It has been over twenty years since I was diagnosed with this illness and I don't know how I would cope if I didn't have my relationship with the Lord. He's there when I can't sleep and in the quiet of the night I can pray or read and just enjoy his presence. This is the grace that brings me through and gives me the strength for each day.

Psalm 46:10

'Be still and know that I am God!'

Chapter 17

Isaiah 40:31

'But those who trust in the Lord will find new strength. They will soar high on wings like eagles. They will run and not grow weary. They will walk and not faint.' (NLT)

Every day I need God's word. When circumstances are closing in on me and I feel suffocated. When loneliness covers me like a dark shadow and I'm crying from the inside out. This is the time to hide in my relationship with God. He is the one I run to. In him I find new strength. I surrender myself to him and my trust and hope is in him. In worship, my spirit begins to soar like the eagles, and I know the freedom I have in Him. Drawing strength, experiencing his love and care, gives me what I need to face the day. I love this verse in Isaiah. It's the solution to my need, it's the direction to whatever will come my way today. I love the Passion translation also.

Isaiah 40:31

'But those who wait for Yahweh's grace will experience divine strength. They will rise up on soaring wings and fly like eagles, run their race without growing weary, and walk through life without giving up.'

So many times, I have felt like giving up. When life becomes too much. When the burdens are just that bit too heavy and I have no strength left. There is nothing like being in God's presence and worshipping, laying down the problems and the worries that get too much. My Lord already knows what I'm going to say before I say it.

He already knows all about the burdens I'm carrying. And it's in this place I can lay them down. It's here that I experience a lightness in my spirit because he knows what I need. He knows the answers to the problems. He doesn't always tell me all the answers because I don't need to know everything at once. He gives me what I need at that moment. He becomes my covering in place of loneliness. I am secure in him because I can trust him for the answers. I can rely on him to work things out for me.

When my husband died, suddenly my world became a smaller and lonelier place. I didn't have a career to go back to and I faced health problems daily. At times I felt afraid. I would become overwhelmed when I realised I was on my own now. I have an amazing family and I love them more than life, but they also have jobs and families. I know they are always there for me if I need them, but I try not to need them. I want them to get on with their lives and enjoy what they are doing. My husband was the closest person to me and now he is gone. I remember the shock I felt when he became ill because he rarely had a cold. When we were told it was terminal cancer, we were devastated. In order to cope, I had to rely on God for strength. Sometimes during a painful situation, I feel like I'm on the outside of it, looking in. I can see then what I need to do to help in every way I can.

One of the things that helps me to cope with anything is going for a drive and then parking the car and just talking to God. Sometimes it can be a tearful conversation, but he is there with me, he is my strength and with every fibre of my being I worship him. My life changed after Billy died in so many ways. In a practical way, there was still the everyday things to be done but he was no longer here to help me.

The bills still had to be paid but my income had halved, the car still needed an MOT, but Billy wasn't here to see to that. Every single day was a new learning experience. Even those days when I felt overcome with grief, when giving up on life seemed like a good option, I kept going. Grief is like going through a long tunnel and there seems to be no end to the heartbreak. Depression would swamp me and there were so many dark days when I longed for light to break through. At its worst, I didn't want to live anymore. What was the point? I wasn't sleeping, I didn't want to eat. I just want the pain to end. For such a long time, I couldn't see beyond the day I was living in. There was no tomorrow or next week and I had no plans for my future. I missed my husband, and my parents were also dead, I felt like an orphan! Okay, I know that sounds dramatic, but my parents and my husband were important relationships in my life and within nine years they were gone. Any plans I'd had for a career was long gone and I felt I was surviving, not living!

I was treading on dangerous ground. I knew it was time to see the doctor and I was prescribed an antidepressant. This type of drug can also help with nerve pain, so it helped me. My mind and my body needed to rest, and it was good to close my eyes at night and sleep for a few hours. For so long there was no light at the end of this tunnel. It can take a long time. I found the first few years after Billy died to be extremely difficult. Eventually the pain eased, the loss was always there but just not as painful. I began to realise that I still had a life to live. God still had a plan and he hadn't given up on me. He was patient in his love to bring me through the dark times to where I could see that life is still worth living. This was a big realisation for me. Losing my husband was like losing that part of me that loved deeply.

That wound takes a long time to begin to heal and grief leaves its own scar. I became more accepting of my life and the circumstances I was living in and there was renewed hope in my spirit.

There comes a time of moving on and for me I sensed within me a restlessness. I decided it was time to sell up the house and move away. I lived in Belfast at the time and went to a church in Newtownabbey, I also have family that live there. When Billy died, I also had him buried in Carmoney, Newtownabbey. I prayed about selling the house and moving that direction. I drove around Newtownabbey looking at different areas and every day I checked out PropertyPal for houses. I got the 'For Sale' sign put up and I admit, I felt a little nervous at the decision I'd made. After a few months, nothing had changed. Nobody had come to view the house; it was just for sale! Winter arrived and I was ill with a severe chest infection. I hadn't been out for several weeks and at one point I wondered if I would survive the winter. One night I woke up from a sleep and I was struggling with my breathing. I sat up in bed and I began to pray. After a few minutes I felt better and got up to make a cup of tea. I came back to bed and I was reading my bible and I began to pray. I saw myself in a house in Newtownabbey, yet everyone I knew, family and friends, while they were around me, I felt far away, isolated. This wasn't the place for me to go. I was puzzled. I had my heart set on going to Newtownabbey, yet I knew that God was saying no. Taking a big deep breath, I asked him, what I was to do. He reminded me of a time when I was visiting my daughter in Lurgan and on the drive home, I got the thought that I might like to live there. But that's all it was, a thought! Now in the stillness of the night, I asked again, and I got my answer. I was going to Lurgan!

I have found in so many situations that God has a sense of humour and he has blessed me with a crazy sense of humour that gets me through so much. When I woke the next morning and I remembered I was going to Lurgan, I thought he was joking. Sure, I had all these plans to go the opposite way. Yet, I knew in my heart I had heard him clearly. I was concerned about the sale of my house because the property market had fallen badly, and my house was going into negative equity. I also needed to have a house to go to in Lurgan and a church.

I had to face the upheaval of leaving this home that had so many memories of my marriage to Billy, not all them were good but they weren't all bad either.

We had lived in this house for years and there was so much stuff to sort out. I wasn't sure I was up for it, yet I knew it was the right thing to do. The sale sign had been up for quite a while and nothing seemed to be happening. With the property market being the way, it was, no one seemed interested in buying. I decided to let the house go through an auction and I'd get as much as possible for it. I still had a mortgage to pay off when it sold, and I needed money to move.

First, I wanted to look for a place to rent in Lurgan. Praise God for the internet. I saw a house I liked and phoned to make an appointment to see it. Next, I needed a church. There are quite a lot in the Lurgan area. I found Emmanuel church in Lurgan and I liked it. It was one place I would visit when I moved.

I began packing up boxes, clearing out stuff for the dump and things for the charity shop. There was so much stuff and I was surprised at how much work was involved sorting through it. Things I had forgotten about, that were stored in a box and I got a surprise when I opened it. I found lots of photographs and magazines that I'd kept, that were now years old! It took weeks to sort stuff and begin to pack. I had lots of books and notebooks and dozens of pens. I didn't realise I was such a hoarder! Each room had three piles of stuff, charity shop, dump and keep. The keep stuff then had to be packed. As I packed the boxes, I decided to put them in the workshop and there would be more space in the house. My idea was a good one, but the workshop would have to be cleared out first.

When it came to sorting Billy's workshop, I was very emotional. There were tools in there the way Billy had left them. I rarely went into the workshop after he died, now I had to.

On his workbench were screwdrivers, a hammer and lots of nuts and bolts. His toolbox sat on the floor where he'd left it and as I stood there, in my mind I could see him working at something. He loved that workshop even though it always seemed to be a mess. I remember telling him that I could put nice little curtains on the windows and the look on his face was enough! There would be no fancy curtains in his domain. It felt strange packing it all away. I thought of the time when he had the motorbike, he loved Betsy and there were a couple of motorbike helmets on the floor. He also used the workshop when he was repairing things and there were still some old parts lying around on the floor and on the workbench. It felt strange as I looked at the place that had been so much a part of Billy's life and now it was just a workshop because he wasn't here anymore. I was sad and I cried as I began to sort through stuff, knowing it was being cleared away for the last time. I grieved for what used to be, and although I felt that pain in my heart, I knew that I was doing the right thing. I couldn't move on with my life while clinging to what used to be. It took days to clean the place and I had to laugh when I saw how clean the floor was and the work bench all tidied. It was never like that when Billy was here. I wonder what he would have thought about it now!

I began to store the packed boxes from the house into the workshop and it made such a difference. There was so much more space in the house, and I wondered how Billy and I had lived with all that stuff! With the boxes out of the way, bags of other stuff taken to the charity shop, I could see the progress I was making. I'd also hired a small skip for stuff that had to be taken to the dump, mostly from Billy's workshop. There were still old washing machines that he had taken parts off and a few broken fridges. They all went into the skip. I felt good when all the work was done, and the rubbish cleared out. It made me feel like I had a new beginning and the clearing out was necessary.

Moving in the opposite direction also meant leaving the church I had been in for twelve years. Jordan Victory Church had been an amazing place to be. I was taught so much there, and I got to know a lot of people.

My last Sunday was emotional for me as I said goodbye to friends and my Pastors, Lewis and Gwen Smith. I will always be grateful for the love and support I received from them throughout my time there. They had helped me so much when Billy was ill and supported me after he died. Lewis had taken the service at Billy's funeral and so many people from the church had been there too. Saying goodbye to what is familiar in my life is difficult and I was sad to leave my church, but goodbyes are part of the process of moving on, although there were tears.

I'd got a house to rent in Lurgan and finally it was time to move. In our family, a house move is a family affair. Colin drove a large van. Paul came with him to do the moving and the three grandsons were there to help carry things. At the

Lurgan end was Julie and her boys, ready and waiting at the new house. Roisin would follow later with food supplies.

It took a while to clear out the house but eventually the van was packed, and they were on their way to Lurgan. I had smaller stuff to pack in my car and check I'd taken everything. Walking back into the house, it was so quiet and empty, and it echoed. I went upstairs and checked the bedrooms and as I closed the doors one last time, I felt very emotional. In every room I had a memory that flashed across my mind. Downstairs the kitchen and living room were empty and clean and I felt sad that this was the end of another chapter in my life. The end of the years I'd spent here with Billy and now I was closing the door on that. I walked down the back path and into the workshop and I had to smile. I had brushed the place and it was clean and I realised I'd never seen it this clean before. I shut the door and walked away. Coming back into the house I closed the back door and locked it, closed the living room door and walked down the hall. Part of me wanted to linger but it was over now, and it was time to go. I opened the front door and, in my heart, said goodbye and stepped outside. I shut the door for the last time. I said goodbye to my neighbours who I'd known for a long time and there were more tears.

I got into my car and as I drove away, I felt that familiar pain in my heart, but I knew I had made the right decision.

Driving up the motorway towards Lurgan it was raining, I was crying and feeling very emotional. A few miles up the road the rain stopped, the sun came out and as I drove, I suddenly got the feeling that everything would be okay. The hardest part was over me and now I had the rest of my life ahead of me. I praised the Lord as I drove. Now Lord, for a new adventure.

A few weeks after I moved to my new house, it was time to visit Emmanuel church. That Sunday morning it was sunny, and I drove through the town and into the church car park. I felt a little apprehensive as I walked into this new place. I needn't have worried. Everyone was friendly and I enjoyed the worship and the sermon and by the end, I knew I'd found my new church family and Emmanuel became my spiritual home. God amazes me the way in which he works things out. He doesn't take me out of situations but through them and he has brought me through so much. Now I had a new beginning in a new place, and I felt like I'd come home.

Psalm 9:1-2

I will praise you, Lord, with all my heart; I will tell of all the marvellous things you have done. I will be filled with joy because of you. I will sing praises to your name, O' Most High.

Chapter 18

It takes a long time to come to terms with living alone. I always liked my own company but sometimes I felt lonely. For a while I'd been thinking about getting a dog. I'd never had a dog of my own. I was usually a cat person. For me to even think about having a dog was unusual but I found myself looking on the internet at dog rescue centres and wondering what breed of dog would be best for me. I'd prayed about this for a long time too. It maybe sounds strange saying that I prayed about getting a dog, but I talk to God about everything else. I knew having a dog would be a new experience for me and I had to be sure it was the right thing to do. Once I'd prayed about it, I believed God had a wee dog for me that needed a home and needed to be loved and cared for. Although at times I felt that way about myself!

My friend Sharon and I were on the internet one afternoon, looking for dogs. She saw a picture of one that needed to be rehomed. I phoned up but was told that someone else was taking the dog. I was disappointed but remembered I was trusting God for my new pet. A week later I got a phone call to say that the dog still needed a home if I wanted it. It was arranged for the dog to be brought to me.

The night that Molly walked into my house I knew she was mine. She was a white westie, cute as anything and I fell in love. She was gorgeous. I loved taking care of her, walking her, playing with her and she loved being on my bed. She was my wee bear, all white and fluffy.

I soon got to know her personality and how stubborn she could be when she wanted something. I spoilt her and she knew she had me where she wanted me. At Christmas I bought her toys and wrapped them up and placed them under the tree. She loved ripping off the paper the next morning. She had lots of toys. She also loved television and she and I would curl up on my recliner chair at night. Her favourite programme was Paul O'Grady, For the Love of Dogs. She would stand in front of the television on her back legs, with her front paws on the TV unit and watch the doggies. The first time she saw it, she couldn't understand when the show was over where the dogs went so she ran behind the television looking for them.

Molly was great company for me and as it was just the two of us, she followed me all over the house. The family loved her too and my grandchildren thought she was so funny. She loved to be the centre of attention and they spoilt her.

My friend Sharon also had a dog, Freya and she and Molly would play together. They knew where the treat cupboard was in my kitchen and they would go and sit there until I got them their treats. My friends George and Ruth loved Molly and they looked after her if I had to go somewhere and I didn't want her to be on her own. They also spoilt her, and she loved going to their house and running out to their back garden to play.

The reason I'm writing about Molly is because I had never loved a pet like her, and she had been an answer to prayer. What I didn't realise when I got her was that to love a pet also means getting your heartbroken. The depth of love I had for Molly was amazing and she loved me. Molly was two years old when I rehomed her in June 2013. For six years she and I shared a fantastic time together. In January 2019 I noticed Molly didn't seem to be herself. She had begun to limp when she was out walking. I took her to the vet, who thought it might be arthritis in her hips and her spine. She was put on medication. Another month went by and she seemed to be going off her food.

Now I only fed Molly the best, but no matter what I gave her, she would only eat a little. She was tested for diabetes, but the test was negative. A few more weeks went by and she developed an incredible thirst but then she would be sick, I knew she had to go back to the vet. This time she was given an injection and different medication.

I took her home, expecting to see some change by that night but she had the worst night ever. I brought her into my bed and even when she fell asleep, she cried in her sleep. By morning she was too weak to walk. I carried to the car and went back to the vet. This time she was kept in and put on an intravenous drip for fluids while they did tests.

Coming home without her was awful and I couldn't sleep with her out of the house. I phoned the vet first thing the next morning, but they wanted to keep her longer. She had now tested positive for diabetes and she was going to be started on insulin. Once she responded, I could bring her home. I felt relieved, at least this illness would be manageable. I really missed her out of the house, and it was so quiet without her running around. Over the next few days Molly didn't respond to insulin and she was also on antibiotics. Blood tests were taken regularly but Molly was still unstable which meant she had to stay on a drip for fluids because she couldn't cope if she were taken off it. I knew in my heart things were not good and I felt so quiet inside. The vet was giving her another twenty-four hours and if things hadn't changed, then we would need to make the decision to stop treatment and let her go.

I was worried and I felt afraid. I didn't want to be without Molly, she was my wee bear. On Sunday morning I was sitting at home and I'd been praying, it had been so quiet at home and I wondered if this was the way it was going to be. I have a large canvas picture on the wall in the living room. It is of a beautiful meadow, lovely trees and flowers and everything about it is peaceful. As I looked at it, I imagined Molly running free over the meadow, healthy and not limping and I knew in my heart that Molly wasn't coming home.

The phone rang and it was the vet. Molly wasn't responding to any treatment. I made the decision for her to be put to sleep but first I wanted to spend some time with her. Julie drove me to the vets, and we were taken into a room to wait for Molly. She was brought into me, but she looked so ill. Julie stroked her and then she went outside so I could be on my own with her. I held Molly like a baby and talked to her and she knew me but when she looked at me, there was no life in her eyes. After a while, the vet came in and I told him I was ready. I held her as he gave her the injection and very quickly it was over. I was calm throughout but when she died, I was devastated. I kissed her goodbye and we left. She died on 7th April 2019. Over the next few days, I was heartbroken. I never knew what it was like to love a pet like this and the pain of grief when I lost her was devastating.

I had prayed for a dog like Molly and I'd had six years with her, and it was so good. It took a while but eventually I accepted she was gone. Sometimes even now, I look up at my picture in the living room and imagine Molly running through the meadow, healthy and happy.

When I lost Molly, I thought twice about getting another pet. I wasn't sure I could have that connection again with another dog. For several months I did nothing. I missed having a dog and it got a bit lonely at times. I prayed again about a pet. In August I saw a photo of a wee dog on Facebook. I knew looking at him that he was depressed and starved of love.

I sent an email to the rescue centre and then I went to see him. Otis is a small Jack Russell terrier; he was eight years old and had been abandoned. I knew he was the dog for me. When I brought him home, he was so nervous, and I sat with him on my bed all night just holding him. He would hide under the table and only come out when he felt sure of me. If anyone came into the house, he would go back under the table. He slept on my bed at night, even though I'd bought him a new bed. He needed so much reassurance. I would tell that I'd keep him safe. It took weeks for Otis to feel safe and now he is an amazing wee dog. He is the opposite of Molly so another new learning curve for me. We have got to know one another now and I wouldn't be without him. He knows every word I say. I had wondered whether I'd be able to have a connection with another dog, I needn't have worried. I fell in love with Otis and we are happy. I realise that one day I might get my heart broken again but then that's what happens when we love, but it's worth it.

Otis has become secure with me and he is like my shadow, he follows me everywhere. He still sleeps on my bed at night and he likes to cuddle into me as we go to sleep. He is the cutest wee dog. He can still be a little nervous in the car, but he is making progress all the time. When I've been out and I arrive home, he runs to me for a cuddle and I'm so happy with him. Otis now has a home that he feels secure in and he knows he is loved, and I have a lovely wee dog to keep me company. I thank God for Otis because another need has been met in my life.

I pray about everything that concerns me. I prayed about a second dog before I got Otis because I trust God to meet my every need. I was lonely after Molly died and when I met Otis at the rescue centre, I knew this wee dog had been starved of love and affection. In my heart, he was the one for me. I say this because being in a relationship with God means I trust him for his best for me. He knows me better than I know myself and he will meet every need, not just for me, but also for Otis. God doesn't just care about the big things in life, but every detail.

Psalm 138:8

'The Lord will work out his plans for my life – For your faithful love endures forever...'

Philippians 4:19

'And this same God who takes care of me will supply all your needs from his glorious riches, which have been given to us in Christ Jesus.'

God gets me, he knows what I need, and I've been blessed in taking care of Molly and now Otis. Pets give such unconditional love and trust and it's so easy to love them back. Now that has to be a blessing!

Chapter 19

I began this book in order to share my story and the experiences I've had in my relationship with God. From the innocence of childhood when I loved and believed the story of Cinderella to the reality of the different life I have lived.

There has been pain in relationships and the loss of a first marriage to divorce. There has been grief, when I have lost loved ones and the loss of a career and education. Many paths I went down resulted in mental and emotional pain, some through choices I made and some that were caused by others. However, I have also gained so much on my journey through life. I have learnt lessons that were difficult at the time but have helped to develop my character and I have gained wisdom in learning to make the right choices.

I would like to think that I'm now older and wiser, but there will always be new lessons to learn and the Holy Spirit guides me daily in what I'm to do. I think the thread that runs through my story, that I hope you the reader will see, is how I found my identity in my relationship with God. To start out with childlike innocent faith and then move on to religion was one of the most painful times for me and that led to my walking away from Church and from God. It took the next nine years for me to discover that relationship with Jesus Christ is the key to living this life. I surrendered to him with my whole heart. However, then I spent so many years entrenched in religion and striving to be the best I could be. I didn't want to be a disappointment to God, yet, in my human strength, of course I made mistakes. It took a long time for me to realise that God loves me for who I am.

I didn't have to try and make myself shiny and perfect. The problem with striving to be the best is that I focused on what I appeared to be on the outside. I wanted to look like a Christian, whatever that means! I was on this merry-go-round of thinking I was getting it right to continually having to repent because I felt so bad about myself. I eventually got to the place in my relationship with Jesus where I realised that my inner relationship with him was the centre of my life. I could cease from striving and beating myself up. I stepped into freedom and began to see my life with a different perspective.

I have experienced his love so deeply and intimately that I know there is nothing or no one that can compare to him. To try and find happiness and fulfilment in anything or anyone else is futile. When Jesus Christ is the centre of life then there is a rock-solid foundation to build on. It doesn't matter what your status is in life, I'm a widow and I enjoy my single life. When I was in a marriage, I depended on my relationship with Jesus to build on the relationship with my husband. A relationship with Jesus is the sure foundation to build on. He is faithful, trustworthy and never fails and when he is the center of any relationship and life is indeed worth living.

Finding my identity in Him led me on a journey of reading his word and believing what he was telling me. As I grew in relationship and knowledge, I began to see the bigger picture that God sees. The questions I had regarding, who am I? Where did I come from? Who do I belong to? What is my destiny? I had so many questions. So many of my conversions with God begin with, 'We need to have a chat.'

Now I know the biology, I had parents and Mum gave birth to me and I grew up in a family. That's simple. But for me, there have always been deep questions in my spirit. I always knew from childhood that there is more to life than what is obvious! My questions took me to the bible and the scriptures that are alive to me because they speak life and truth and they bring peace and understanding. Reading Psalm 139 is a good place to begin.

Psalm 139:1-7

'O Lord, you have examined my heart and know everything about me. You know when I sit down or stand up. You know my thoughts even when I'm far away. You see me when I travel and when I rest at home. You know everything I do. You know everything I say even before I say it, Lord. You go before me and follow me. You place your hand of blessing on my head. Such knowledge is too wonderful for me, too great for me to understand! I can never escape from your Spirit! I can never get away from your presence!

This is a God who knows me better than I know myself and his hand of blessing upon my life. However, he didn't just know me from birth.

Psalm 139:13-18

You made all the delicate parts, inner parts of my body and knit me together in my mother's womb. Thank you for making me so wonderfully complex! Your workmanship is marvellous – how well I know it. You watched me as I was being formed in utter seclusion, as I was woven in the dark of the womb. You saw me before I was born. Every day of my life was recorded in your book. Every moment was laid out before a single day had passed. How precious are your thoughts about me, O God. They cannot be numbered! I can't even count them; they outnumber the grains of sand! And when I wake up, you are still with me.'

God is my Creator and I'm his child. The sense of belonging that this revelation brought to me was amazing. There is so much more to life when the spirit is awakened and connects with the Creator. Every day is a new beginning and no matter what happens in the day, I know I'm not on my own. My God is with me every minute and in every situation. He is there at the end of the day when I find my rest in him and he watches me as I sleep. However, it took a long time for me to really grasp the reality of being God's child.

I remember a time when I was in my thirties and I was going through a difficult time. I began to doubt just about everything in my life. I was feeling really lost and when I prayed, it was like, heaven was silent. One night I was in bed reading over my bible and not really knowing what I was searching for when I opened at the book of Jeremiah. Glancing down the first chapter, I stopped at verse five and just burst into tears.

Jeremiah 1:5 (N.I.V.)

'Before I formed you in the womb, I knew you, before you were born, I set you apart...'

There had been so many times in my life when I felt that I was one big mistake. That I would always go from one mistake to another and be a big mess with no other purpose than the next mistake and the next wrong choice!

No, No, No!

God was saying, 'BEFORE I FORMED YOU IN THE WOMB, I KNEW YOU...'

He was telling me I wasn't a mistake because he knew me, and he knew me before I was even formed in the womb. God doesn't make mistakes! I was meant to be even though

I often thought that just this once God might have got it wrong! No, God doesn't get it wrong. In Psalm 139 he tells me that he created me in the womb and in Jeremiah 1, he tells that before he even formed me that he knew me.

I realised that I'd been believing the lies of the enemy for far too long. Those lies that told me I was a mess and I'd made so many mistakes that God could never use me. I would just about make into heaven and no more. My mind was tormented with so many lies, and my thoughts affected me mentally and emotionally until I had almost given up on myself and I believed that I was a big let-down to God.

I prayed and repented of believing the lies of the enemy and then I rejoiced because I wasn't a mistake, God loved me as his child and he knew me, and every single day I live he knows me in everything. The security in finding my identity in him is totally life changing. No matter what lies the enemy tried to tell me I know with all my heart, my God made me and has a purpose for my life. I'm his, full stop!

Getting to know Jesus up close and personal is the most intimate, beautiful relationship. I love the stories in the New Testament that tells of the times when Jesus talked to women. In the times that they lived in, women were not treated well, they were not educated, they depended on having a husband in order to have any kind of life and that husband could divorce her for the smallest thing. Yet, along comes Jesus and along comes freedom.

In John 4, he has a conversation with a Samaritan woman which in itself was amazing as Jews and Samaritans didn't talk. I love that this conversation was so honest. Jesus is sitting at a well when this woman comes to get water.

John 4

Soon a Samaritan woman came to draw water and Jesus said to her. 'Please give me a drink?' he was alone at the time because his disciples had gone into the village to buy food. The woman was surprised, for Jews refuse to have anything to do with Samaritans. She said to Jesus, 'You are a Jew and I am a Samaritan woman. Why are you asking me for a drink?'

Jesus replied, 'If you only knew the gift God has for you and who you are speaking to, you would ask me, and I would give you living water.'

But sir, you don't have a rope or a bucket,' she said. 'and this well is very deep. Where would you get this living water? And besides, do you think you're greater than our ancestor Jacob, who gave us this well? How can you offer better water than he and his sons and his animals enjoyed?'

Jesus replied. 'Anyone who drinks this water will soon be thirsty again. But those who drink the water I give will never be thirsty again. It becomes a fresh, bubbling spring within them, giving them eternal life.'

'Please sir,' the woman said, 'give me this water! Then I'll never be thirsty again and I won't have to come here to get water.

'Go and get your husband.' Jesus told her.

'I don't have a husband,' the woman replied.

Jesus said, 'You're right! You don't have a husband – for you have had five husbands, and you aren't even married to the man you're living with now. You certainly spoke the truth!'

'Sir,' the woman said, 'you must be a prophet. So, tell me, why is it that you Jews insist that Jerusalem is the only place of worship, while we Samaritans claim it is here at Mount Gerizim, where our ancestors worshipped?'

Jesus replied. 'Believe me, dear woman, the time is coming when it will no longer matter whether you worship the Father on this mountain or in Jerusalem. You Samaritans know very little about the one you worship, while we Jews know all about him, for salvation comes through the Jews. But the time is coming – indeed it is here

now – when true worshippers will worship the Father in spirit and in truth. The Father is looking for those who will worship him that way. For God is Spirit, so those that worship him must worship him in spirit and in truth.'

The woman said, 'I know the Messiah is coming – the who is called Christ. When he comes, he will explain everything to us.'

Then Jesus said to her, I AM the Messiah.'

I read this and just go, 'Wow.'

This woman had such a long conversation with Jesus, and it changed her life. He loved her, accepted her and revealed himself to her. He doesn't name her because he gave her dignity. The woman went back to her village and told everyone about Jesus and then they came to see for themselves and asked Jesus to stay and he did, for two days. At the end of it, many believed in him.

When I read about the way Jesus treated women, with dignity and respect, love and acceptance, I realise that women's liberation didn't begin in the 1960's, it began with Jesus and continues to this day. Jesus came to free me from everything that binds me, gets in the way of my relationship

179

with him and robs me of destiny. His word is truth and believing in him is the only way forward in life.

John 8:32

And you will know the truth and the truth will set you free. '

Truth and freedom cuts through all the emotional pain that I've experienced in my life and experiencing the love of Christ daily is the wellspring to living.

When I pray, I listen to the small still voice of the Holy Spirit as he guides me. When I read my bible, he directs me through the scriptures and all the answers to life are in him.

Romans 8:1-2

So now there is no condemnation for those who belong to Christ Jesus. And because you belong to him, the power of the life-giving Spirit has freed you. '

I am free, I no longer have to listen to the lies of the enemy that say, I'm not enough, I'll never amount to anything and I've missed out in life. One of the biggest lies that I have had to break through is the lie that tells me that I'm older now and it's too late for me to have my dreams. The lie that says, just settle for what life is now because nothing else is going to change!

NO, NO, NO!

I've only to look at the bible and see for myself that age really doesn't matter to God. Moses was forty when he ran away from Egypt, he was eighty when God appeared to him at the burning bush and told him he was being sent back to Egypt to free the children of Israel. And he was one hundred and twenty when he died.

God is never finished until he says it's over. There are so many examples in scripture that we relate to, yet, for me personally, the older I've got, the lie that came against me, was that I was past doing anything for God. The enemy is a liar. He has been lying from the garden of Eden and he is still lying. As a child of God, I only have to remind him that the blood of Jesus covers me, and God hasn't finished with me yet. The enemy has no authority in my life or over my mind unless I give it to him. This is where I have my battle. I've had those times when depression had me in such a dark place and I've cried out to God. As I have matured in my relationship with him, I now realise Satan is only interested in me because of my relationship with Jesus.

If the enemy can attack my mind, then I get distracted from the things I should be doing. I can lose sight of my dreams and life can become mundane. The simplest way out for me is to pray and praise. Sometimes I put on a CD and sing and eventually I get the victory over the enemy. The Christian life is a battle and I can't go cruising through life thinking the devil is going to overlook me, he's not. I'm in a relationship with Jesus and he defeated the devil on the cross. Jesus bought my freedom, my salvation and all I need to live this life at Calvary. I belong to my Father and all heaven is on my side.

Psalm 91:1-4. 14-16

Those who live in the shelter of the Most High will find rest in the shadow of the Almighty. This I declare about the Lord; He alone is my refuge, my place of safety; he is my God and I trust Him. For he will rescue you from every trap and protect you from deadly disease. He will cover you with his feathers, He will shelter you with his wings. His faithful promises are your armour and protection.

The Lord says, 'I will rescue those who love me. I will protect those who trust in my name. When they call on me, I will answer; I will be with them in trouble. I will rescue and honour them. I will reward them with a long life and give them my salvation.'

Learning to take God at his word and embracing his truth gives me everything I need in life and in him I find my identity and security.

Chapter 20

I've gained so much in knowing Jesus. When I think back to my younger years when I was full of ambition and dreams, I spent my time wondering how I could accomplish all I wanted to do. Now there is nothing wrong with having ambition and there is nothing wrong with having a dream for your life. I still have things that I want to accomplish. The difference is, I'm not depending on me. I'm not depending on how hard I need to strive. I'm depending on my relationship with Jesus, the guidance of the Holy Spirit and the surrender of my heart to him daily.

I used to wonder what my destiny is in life. How do I know what destiny even is? Did I even believe in destiny? So many questions. I'm sure there are times God shakes his head with my endless questions. I've discovered that destiny is something that is already in me. I don't need to go searching for something that appears to be destiny. I find that the desires that have been on my heart since childhood are the seeds of my destiny. Everything I have experienced in life, relationships, jobs, education and various churches I've been involved with, have all been part of my destiny.

Even the times when I made the wrong choices, I experienced a hard learning curve, but my dreams never died. It has been such a learning curve, and nothing is ever wasted with God. I still have dreams and as I get older the dreams get bigger! Watch this space for that one!

I love to write, and I intend to keep writing. I love to talk to people, pray with people and help reach out to those who are hurting. God has brought me through so much pain in my life and brought so much inner healing. I want to be the one who now stands in the gap and prays for those who can't speak for themselves, for those who have been abused, those who have known rejection and those who need to know the love of Jesus Christ in their lives.

In years gone by when most of my jobs were in community and social welfare, I thought when I had to give up work and education due to health issues, then my desire to reach out and help was over. But no, it's not over until God says it's over. My education as an adult was something I enjoyed and when I had to put my books away, I felt so disappointed.

Recently I was reading in the book of Isaiah 58. The chapter talks about fasting and the kind of fasting that God wants.

Isaiah 58:6-9

'No, this is the kind of fasting I want; Free those who are wrongly imprisoned; lighten the burden of those who work for you. Let the oppressed go free and remove the chains that bind people. Share your food with the hungry and give shelter to the homeless. Give clothes to those who need them and do not hide from relatives who need your help. Then your salvation will come like the dawn and your wounds will quickly heal. Your godliness will lead you forward, and the glory of the Lord will protect you from behind. Then when you call, the Lord will answer, 'Yes I am here.' He will quickly reply.

When I read through this passage, I call this is God's plan for social welfare and as Christians we can reach out to those in need.

While we live on this earth there will always be opportunity to help someone along the way. I was glad of the times in my life when I needed help and God placed people in my life to encourage me and help me. I've had times when I needed help for depression, and I had a doctor who understood my pain. I've had counselling and prayer for inner healing and I'm so grateful to God that I've known people who reached out to me and loved me and prayed with me. God knew the areas in my life where I needed help and he placed those in my life that reached out to help me. It's so important for people to realise that God is a good God and he wants each one of us to have the life he intended for us.

As I write this, we have just come through lockdown, due to Covid-19. This year has been a new learning curve for everyone. At times I struggled because I missed my family and I missed going to church. At other times I enjoyed the rest and the quiet. It was like God was resetting my life and I needed to go with the flow of it. This year has been uncertain for many people. Just about every area in life has been affected. People have lost loved ones because of this virus and even funerals had to be different. At times I have felt distressed and more than ever I've had to learn to be still and know that God is still God.

Lockdown brought changes to the way I see myself. I learnt to take better care of me. While I struggle with health issues, there have been times when I have pushed to do things and ended up in more pain. Times when I ignored the fatigue and then hadn't the strength to take a shower. I also spent a lot of time reading and writing in my journal and staying in the shelter of God's care. This is refreshing and much needed for body, soul and spirit.

We are now learning to move on, and people have begun to go back to work and children to school, yet there is still the need to stay safe. 2020 has been an unsettling year for everyone, but it is in these hard times that I lean into God and believe he will bring us through this. What has happened this year hasn't come as a surprise to God, and he is not in a panic over it.

I believe his words and his promises and I'm still secure. It's at times like this that I've had to learn that God is true. In standing back from a situation and looking from the outside in, I see the chaos and the distress that lockdown had brought. Who ever thought people would nearly fight each other over a packet of toilet rolls! Lockdown was frightening at first, but it is then that my faith becomes my shield. God knows the end from the beginning, and I trust him to bring us through this.

This year has gone so quickly, and nothing has felt normal and I have been unsettled and out of my routine. I have also sensed changes in my spirit, an unsettling of what has been familiar to me. It was like my roots were being shaken and when this happens to me, I know I'm being shaken for a reason. I like to be comfortable and settled and while lockdown has done the opposite to me, I was hoping to return to what I thought was my normal. Yet, I sensed that I wouldn't go back to what was familiar. I had been a member of Emmanuel church for eight years and I loved it. I was content to be there until God called me home. I loved and respected my Pastors, Philip and Lorraine Emersion and the church leadership. I loved the women's fellowship, Maureen Ross Jones taught us every Tuesday and I learnt so much. As a widow I always felt cared for by my church family and I embraced that love and care. Yet, for several months I sensed that a season in my life was coming to an end.

Ecclesiastes 3:1-8

For everything there is a season, and a time for every activity under heaven. A time to be born and a time to die. A time to plant and a time to harvest. A time to like and a time to heal. A time to tear down and a time to build up. A time to laugh and a time to cry. A time to grieve and a time to dance. A time to scatter stones and a time to gather stones. A time to embrace and a time to turn away. A time to search and a time to quit searching. A time to tear and a time to mend. A time to be quiet and a time to speak. A time to love and a time to hate. A time for war and a time for peace.

I know that in life I have seasons of change. There is a time for everything. But, before I can go forward, I need to be still in the moment and realise that there is indeed an ending. For a time, I felt low in spirit, I didn't want to accept change because I like to be comfortable! I struggled so much, and I prayed even more. I found the decision I had to make difficult, yet I knew in my spirit that I was moving to a different place.

I felt sad that I was having to say goodbye to Emmanuel. When I moved to Lurgan in 2012, I remember the first Sunday I had walked into church. I was nervous yet excited that I was living in a new place and now I had found a new church. I was made so welcome and right from that first Sunday, I had that sense of belonging. Now, eight years later, my sense of belonging was being shaken. Sometimes I just know in my spirit when such a massive change is coming. My question to God was simple, 'Where are you taking me too?'

I have friends that took me to visit their church and I knew that this would be my new place. Before I could make a commitment there, I first had to honour my church leadership of Emmanuel Church and I contacted my Pastor. I am glad that I left with a blessing and that their hearts and doors are always open to me. I think it is important to give honour to my church leadership and I pray God continues to bless Emmanuel Church abundantly. Regardless of where we worship the Lord, we are family and always will be.

I now belong to Portadown Christian Centre and I'm enjoying it. It takes time to settle in a new place and get to know new people, but I have been made so welcome by everyone. Pastors George and Irene Elliott and the people there have an amazing vision for the new building that is in the process of being finished. This place will be for the people that God will bring to it. A place where people will find salvation and relationship with Jesus Christ and a place where the hurt and wounded will find inner healing and wholeness. A place that will embrace and love everyone who walks through the doors.

Jeremiah 3:15 (KJV)

'And I will give you pastors according to mine heart, which shall feed you with knowledge and understanding.'

I pray for my church leadership, past and present because God has set them in place, and they have a responsibility and accountability to God for his flock. I feel it's so important to recognise that they need prayer and support to carry out the ministry they have been called to.

I'm excited at what God is doing in my life as I begin to put down roots in this new place. I believe I should bloom where I'm planted, and this is my time of planting and there will be a time of harvest.

When Jesus was on this earth, he taught his disciples and prepared them for the time when he would no longer be with them. I love the gospel of John as it shows Jesus in his love for people, how he taught his disciples and his relationship with his Father.

When my life needed direction, I remember opening at John 14.

John 14:1-4,5

'Don't let your hearts be troubled. Trust in God and trust also in me. There is more than enough room in my Father's home. If this were not so, would I have told you that I am going to prepare a place for you? When everything is ready, I will come and get you, so that you will always be with me where I am. And you know the way to where I am going.'

Jesus told them. 'I am the way, the truth and the life. No one can come to the Father except through me.'

John 14:15-17

'If you love me, obey my commandments. And I will ask the Father, and he will give you another Advocate, who will never leave you. He is the Holy Spirit who leads into all truth.'

When Jesus was talking to the disciples, he knew what was ahead of him and he tried to prepare these men who had been with him throughout his ministry. He loved them and they had to be prepared for the ministry that was ahead of them.

John 14:25-27

'I am telling you these things now while I am still with you. But when the Father sends the Advocate as my representative – that is, the Holy Spirit – he will teach you everything and will remind you of everything I have told you.

I am leaving you with a gift – peace of mind and heart. And the peace I give you is a gift the world cannot give. So, don't be troubled or afraid.'

Jesus offers us the same invitation. A relationship with Him and peace of mind and heart. His love is amazing, and the Holy Spirit teaches us how to live each day and have the best life. I will always remember that day in 1979 when he spoke to me.

Isaiah 43:1

But now, O Jacob, listen to the Lord who created you. O Israel, the one who formed you says, 'Do not be afraid, for I have ransomed you, I have called you by name; you are mine.'

I heard him and I have never regretted saying, 'Yes God.'

God loves me totally and unconditionally. It was because of love that he sent his son Jesus. He thought I was worth it. In accepting Jesus as Lord, I embarked on an adventure that is life changing. To step into a relationship with him is to embrace the greatest love of all. Life is never the same since I fell in love with Him, he will never break my heart, his love is for eternity. God is faithful, he keeps his promises and I have come to know him as my Father, Papa, my Lord, my Saviour, a Husband and Friend. Everything I need in life comes from him and he sustains me, walks me through life with grace and shelters me in the storm. His love covers me, and I am safe in his care.

Jesus gave me a new beginning to a different kind of life and I'm forever thankful.

John 3:16 'For God loved the world so much that he gave his one and only Son, so that everyone who believes in him will not perish but have eternal life.'

Dear Reader

I hoped you have enjoyed reading my story. So many times, in my life I tried to do things my way and then wondered why it didn't work out. Sometimes I had to go round the long way, thinking I was taking a shortcut! My revelation came through painful experience yet, it was a life changing experience. I will never forget the day when God said:

'I have called you by name, you are mine.' (Isaiah 43:1-2)

That was the beginning of finding my identity in God and knowing what it is like to be his child, to be loved and cherished by the One who created the universe. To get to know Jesus as Saviour and Lord and to be up close and personal as I journey through life. It's the best way to live.

Whoever you are and whatever your circumstances, God loves you and wants you to know you are his child. You don't have to struggle with life when there is one who wants to carry you. No matter what situation you find yourself in, let me assure you that there is nothing that God doesn't already know about. See, none of us can hide from him! He longs for each of us to know him and accept his Son, Jesus as Saviour and Lord of our lives.

My life has purpose and I'm thankful that God has brought me to where I am today. I couldn't have got here without him!

God Bless You

Christine Holmes

Psalm 103:1-6 (The Passion Translation)

With my whole heart, with my whole life, and my innermost being, I bow in wonder and love before you, the Holy God.

Yahweh, you are my soul's celebration. How could I forget the miracles of kindness you've done for me?

You kissed my heart with forgiveness, in spite of all I've done. You've healed me inside and out from every disease. You've rescued me from hell and saved my life. You've crowned me with love and mercy and made me a king.

You satisfy my every desire with good things. You've supercharged my life so that I soar again like a flying eagle in the sky.

You're a God who makes things right, giving justice to the defenseless.

Printed in Great Britain
by Amazon

63906060R00119